TREASURY OF ALPHABETS

AND LETTERING

JAN TSCHICHOLD

Treasury of Alphabets and Lettering

A SOURCE BOOK

OF THE BEST LETTER FORMS

OF PAST AND PRESENT

FOR

SIGN PAINTERS

GRAPHIC ARTISTS

COMMERCIAL ARTISTS

TYPOGRAPHERS

PRINTERS · SCULPTORS

ARCHITECTS

AND SCHOOLS OF ART

AND DESIGN

W·W·NORTON & COMPANY
New York · London

A NORTON PROFESSIONAL BOOK
"MEISTERBUCH DER SCHRIFT"
ENGLISH TRANSLATION BY WOLF VON ECKARDT
COPYRIGHT © 1952, 1965 BY RAVENSBURGER BUCHVERLAG,
OTTO MAIER GMBH
INTRODUCTION BY BEN ROSEN, COPYRIGHT © 1992 BY DESIGN PRESS
PRINTED IN THE UNITED STATES OF AMERICA

Library of Congress Cataloging-in-Publication Data
Tschichold, Jan, 1902–1974.
[Meisterbuch der Schrift. English]
Treasury of alphabets and lettering : a source book of the best
letter forms of past and present for sign painters, graphic artists,
commercial artists, typographers, printers, sculptors, architects,
and schools of art and design / Jan Tschichold.
p. cm.
Translation of: Meisterbuch der Schrift.
Includes bibliographical references and
ISBN 0-393-70197-2
1. Type and type-founding. 2. Printing-Specimens.
3. Alphabets. 4. Lettering. I. Title.
Z250. T883   1995   94-35996
686.2'24-dc20   CIP

W. W. Norton & Company, Inc., 500 Fifth Avenue, New York, NY 10110
W. W. Norton & Company, Ltd., 10 Coptic Street, London WC1A 1PU

1 2 3 4 5 6 7 8 9 0

CONTENTS

FOREWORD

B ASED on decades of study, this source book for lettering men,
graphic designers, lithographers and related professions should
serve not just the moment. The letters I have ultimately selected
have stood the test of severe scrutiny. We may therefore hope that,
for decades to come they will also stand the test of time. The plates
offer the familiar as well as the unknown; they are immediately useful as well as inspirational; they contain letters for students as well
as for masters. All of them contribute to a true culture of letters and
their application.

For the publishers, as well as myself, I wish to thank the following
type foundries which have cheerfully supplied type specimens set to
my specifications for some of the plates:

Bauersche Gießerei, Frankfurt am Main;
Schriftgießerei H. Berthold AG, Berlin SW 61;
Bundesdruckerei, Berlin SW 68;
B. S. Cron, Esq., Kew, Surrey;
Fonderies Deberny & Peignot, Paris;
Lettergieterij Joh. Enschedé en Zonen, Haarlem;
Fonderie Typographique Française, Paris;
Haas'sche Schriftgießerei, Münchenstein bei Basel;
Linotype and Machinery Limited, London;
The Monotype Corporation Limited, London;
Museum für die Geschichte der Stadt Leipzig, Leipzig;
Direktor Rudolf Ottmann, Nürnberg;
Stephenson, Blake & Co., Sheffield;
Schriftgießerei D. Stempel AG, Frankfurt am Main.

Jan Tschichold Hon. R.D.I.

INTRODUCTION

Designers of my acquaintance go through books, articles, and graphic design publications in search of prods to their imagination. They seek inspiration through information from past performance, current comments, and future predictions about their chosen discipline. Instinctively they know that effective visual communication demands the courage to experiment with emerging stylistic trends that reflect current attitudes and technical approaches. They also know that a sound background in their subject can help lend authenticity to their work and perspective to their point of view. "Past is prologue" was true in the tracing pad years, and it is no less true in the era of the computer.

Increasingly, these designers and other readers of graphics publications encounter some of the ideas and work produced by Jan Tschichold, a man who exerted significant influence over the graphic design output of Europe and the Americas of the twentieth century. His particular talents were largely focused on type and typography.

Tschichold (1902–74) was a man with a love for letters. The son of a sign painter and lettering artist, he could be said to have come by his fixation naturally. According to an excellent study by Ruari McLean, titled *Jan Tschichold: typographer*, Tschichold at first thought he would become an artist but, for practical reasons, decided on a career as a drawing instructor. Quite early in his life, while assisting his father, he developed insights and an understanding of letterforms and techniques – and the die was cast. While still in his preteen years, he would redesign letters on signs and display types that displeased him, a practice many graphic designers recall from their youth with a tolerant smile. And so it seemed that one way or another, his life work would involve type and lettering.

Seeking to inform himself while still in his teens, he enthusiastically studied related arts and skills. His interests included calligraphy, engraving, etching, wood engraving, and bookbinding. In his ardent pursuit of classics in the fields of lettering, calligraphy, and typography, the idea of working with type and type design as a vocation seems to have made an indelible impression on his mind. Later, as a practicing typographer, type designer, and graphic designer, Tschichold also taught and wrote persuasively about the principles and practice of good typography at a time when the "new" typography was still mainly theory. In *Die neue Typographie*, a book by Tschichold published in 1928, he set forth the principles of the contemporary German design movement of the same name.

Before 1940, avant-garde "commercial art" (read "visual communication") in the United States was still in a relatively early stage of development. It had not yet emerged as the pervasive craft we know it to be today. This is not to suggest that nothing seminal or of creative value was produced. There were exceptions. But a generation of commercial artists felt the dampening effect of a typical makeshift workstation during the 30s and 40s, set up in an obscure corner behind a door, next to an erratic radiator, while struggling with impossible deadlines. Commercial artists were viewed as interchangeable parts, readily replaced appendages to agencies, service studios, newspapers, magazines, and printshops, where, all too often, they became gofers to strippers and workhorses to sales personnel. At many ad agencies they were subjected to constant pressures to speed up their production and compromise their output. This ragtag cadre often worked for a pittance and was kept as far from the client as possible. Yet because their essential skills and talents were indispensable, they were tolerated. Graphic designers survived the years prior to 1950 as ubiquitous loose cannons.

In 1940, Will Burtin, recently arrived in the United States, taught classes in graphic design at Pratt Institute. He was an admirer of Tschichold and like Tschichold believed in the power of skilled graphic representation of ideas. He advanced the notion that, for the graphic design community of the time, Tschichold's was a pioneering message that worked to empower emerging design disciplines. To Tschichold, type and typographic design were fundamental links in the visual communications chain, serious pursuits in which the designer stands between raw information and the audience toward which it is directed; he held that enhancement or blurring of the strength and clarity of a message is a reflection of the skill, experience, education, and creative powers of the designer.

In the late 40s, the postwar surge of economic power in the United States demanded improved effectiveness in visual communications to proclaim its latent strength. Graphic designers, a number of whom had come to the United States to escape the turmoil in Europe, responded with a well-documented, monumental burst of creative energy. Foreign influence was such that William Golden of CBS, whose contributions to advertising and promotion design were legendary, said in an address to the Type Directors Club of New York, in 1959, "If there is such a thing as a 'New American Typography,' surely it speaks with a foreign accent." Whatever its accent, the new graphic design output functioned, in a way, like an international visual identification program, announcing the postwar emergence of American power, influence, and economic expansion.

Tschichold seemed to anticipate the pervasive flood of information that arrived in the wake of World War II, offering both promise and challenge to the new breed of graphic designers. Admittedly, not every message would be of earth-shaking importance, but many would have significance and should not be fumbled.

Unprecedented growth of the national economy was at the heart of this expanded role for the American design industry. But there were other significant factors at work. For some time fresh insights and attitudes about graphic design had been taking root in the hearts and minds of European and American designers. Jan Tschichold was prominent among them.

Tschichold's message, within its timeframe, was innovative and cast a long shadow. In his study of the subtle forms of early manuscripts and derivative lettering and type, he recognized the presence of high levels of craftsmanship and originality that, in his view, rivaled painting, sculpture, and architecture. He closely observed the development of visual communication practice in Europe and America, a study he considered indispensable to any designer of alphabets. It was only after having made these observations that one might presume the "entitlement" to redesign or in any way modify civilization's store of accepted alphabet designs. Tschichold deplored and even ridiculed "personal expression" in graphic design. He considered that it too often masked a lack of disciplined skills and professional craftsmanship. Further, it was no excuse for what he considered the disfiguring effects of poor design. The "renaissance man in a hurry" was not his idea of solid achievement.

Tschichold's writing is often hortative, with a dogmatic tone that is highly unpopular in the United States. This quality may have interfered with broader acceptance of his work and ideas among American designers, to whom some of his dictums seem too confining. Examples may be seen in his recommendations that "it is better to position a column of type closer to the right than to the left side of a page," or that "the right margin should be wider than the space between words." There are those to whom this would read like the brand of pedantry that goes to great lengths to confirm that a jackass has ears. Perceptive readers will have little difficulty finding some ideas and admonitions that no longer apply. But the reader should not allow this to cloud the larger issue of Tschichold's relentless and largely productive efforts to uplift the disciplines that comprise effective visual communications. To do so would be to throw the baby out with the bath water. In time Tschichold became more tolerant, saving his most severe criticism for his own work.

When the graphic design output of the 30s and 40s is viewed from today's perspective, the dimensions of Tschichold's contributions are more readily appreciated. Among the first to foster the perception of designers as significant partners in the communication process, he also cast designers in the role of socially responsible, creative practitioners, dedicated to achieving excellence in their field. His insistence on background knowledge, experience, and the drive to develop broad aesthetic judgment in related fields imparted undeniable merit to his teaching and writing. Some of his specific statements may be debatable, but his point of view retains a universal ring and carries as much weight today as when first offered. Clearly, his attitude lends stature and reinforces the self-esteem of all who work seriously in graphic design.

Useful insights to his thinking may be obtained by reading the "Penguin Composition Rules," to be found in McLean's book. The rules were established as part of a major redesign project for Penguin Books in 1947. Executed in England, this is one of the early examples of what later came to be known as a "visual identification program." During the years immediately following World War II, graphic design in England was in the process of reconstruction, having been set back by the urgencies of the long war. The Penguin project had considerable influence in London and abroad, in that it reaffirmed Tschichold's position on the significance and reach of the graphic designer. It served to consolidate the idea that the skill and inventiveness with which information is delivered is in itself a statement about a given product. For the high information-dispensing society waiting in the wings, this project was one more reason to value the contribution of a dedicated graphic designer who could somehow magically impart a desired "image," a specific kind of "visual identity" to a product, service or idea and do so at will. Thus were these new buzzwords born.

To students and designers alike Tschichold defined his views of the scope and value of visual communications. He held that designers must put aside personal expression, which he viewed as an egotistical intrusion. Personal expression (read "inspiration") would materialize by accumulating knowledge, applying experience, and striving for excellence. It should not be glued on like veneer. One should not allow a preconceived personal style to dominate one's work to the extent that job after job is forced into the designer's format, whether that format is appropriate or not. Lettering, type, and typography are elements of high craftsmanship. They should be circumspectly approached through a mastery of professional skills, a sense of responsibility for maintaining high performance levels, and dedication to one's discipline. It was the message that should come through, not the designer's ego.

To achieve these levels one must first develop sensitivity to the principles of design, awareness of the historical continuity of visual communications, familiarity with the craft of creating calligraphic and drawn letterforms, type as an extension of written alphabets, and the relationship of type to printing. To bring this list up to speed today, the capability of working effectively with digital type should be added.

Today, designers can readily accept this approach. They are concerned with finding a strong "graphic idea," and tend to express impatience with the minutiae of weight variations in a rule-formed border or two millimeters' difference in margin designations advocated by Tschichold in what might have been a dyspeptic mood. Despite his freely offered "right and wrong" ways to solve design problems, he remains a man of lofty principles who, by nature, was a stickler for detail, one who might readily share the point of view of master architect Mies van der Rohe declaring, "God is in the details."

Designers always have a choice between hokey pursuits and solid achievements, whatever they labor in. It is refreshing to see evidence of the abiding interest, the dedication and perseverance of Jan Tschichold in his lifelong search to enhance the discipline of his choice.

Type and typography have advanced considerably since this book was first published in 1963. Taste changes as it rides new technology into modern times. The role of the graphic designer and typographer has broadened along the lines advocated by Tschichold. A recently maturing phenomenon will soon be seen to exert great influence on the users of type in the 90s. For better or for worse, desktop publishing is here, making it possible for anyone to set type!

What this may come to mean for type development in this decade remains to be seen. Tschichold witnessed the shift from typography with metal type to typographic design on layout pads. He observed the early digitization of type and the advent of computers. He also saw the evolution of designers from pencil pushers to basic contributors at every level of visual communication. As a young adult, Tschichold centered his concerns on traditional metal type practice. He seized what he saw as unexploited opportunities to upgrade type and graphic design. He searched instinctively and extensively for a method of achieving a better quality of typographic practice for machine-age typography. He was at the height of his powers when the age of electronics was ushered in. Computerization, technical strides in photographic technology, and the early advent of both phototypesetting and digitization were on the horizon by midcentury. He embraced these technological advances. One of his last significant commissions was to design a new face, which he based on Garamond. Called Sabon, the new type was adapted for use on early phototypesetting equipment. Sabon, now digitized, has achieved classic status since its introduction in 1968.

The digitization of types has resulted in considerable change in the appearance of some faces; for others, the transition is virtually imperceptible. New typefaces are beginning to flood the market. No doubt the universal spread of the formidable personal computer will shape many aspects of turn-of-the-century life, not the least of which will be type design.

Today's designers continue the search for new ways to integrate type design and typographic practice within the framework of currently pervasive digital and laser technology. For the serious student of graphic design, the admonitions of Jan Tschichold loom large and appropriate: make a continuing study of the history of human endeavor, develop sensitivity to the broad creative contributions of the arts, and focus on the character of good letterform, type, and typography as they evolved through the centuries.

Because typesetting is now possible for virtually everyone, we shall continue to see a rash of new styles, unpredictable forms, modified alphabets, different typographic principles, and aesthetically unique applications of type emerge. This convergence may produce an era of innovative typographic practice, where new forms are adapted to traditional models in ways not seen before. Perhaps the best is yet to come. And it will be no surprise to find that the best of the new typography will mirror the disciplined ideas and approach that, to a large extent, can be found in the work of Jan Tschichold.

In the interest of fine letterform development, he compiled this book, among others. The contents of this *Treasury* is presented here in precisely the way he designed it, with this introduction the one minor exception. It represents his concept of a treasure trove of impeccable models for professional and aspiring designers who work with type.

Ben Rosen

LETTERING AS A WORK OF ART

OOD lettering demands three things: – (1) Good letters. A beautiful letter form must be selected which is appropriate to the purpose it is to serve and to the lettering technique to be used. – (2) Good design in all details. This calls for well balanced and sensitive letter spacing and word spacing which takes the letter spacing into account. – (3) A good layout. An harmonious and logical arrangement of lines is essential. None of these three demands can be neglected. Good lettering requires as much skill as good painting or good sculpture. Although it serves a definite purpose and not necessarily eternity, good lettering is equal to the fine arts. The designer of letters, whether he be a sign painter, a graphic artist or in the service of a type foundry, participates just as creatively in shaping the style of his time as the architect or poet.

Good letters are rare. Most of the letters we see about us are ugly, inadequate, or erratic. This is not an exaggeration. The reason for the shamefully low quality of most lettering on our city streets and buildings is the lack of good models. There are only a few good source books and these are difficult or impossible to obtain. The readily available ones are often of poor quality, hastily thrown together without adequate knowledge. The models are hardly ever based directly on the original sources. They are third-, fourth-, and fifth-hand imitations which have become increasingly worse along the way, even if the original source was good. The talented lettering man is thus inadequately equipped. Schools often teach letter forms that are far from the best and seem satisfied with mediocre and unskilled performance. Most lettering men do not even know genuine, beautiful letter forms since they have no access to them. No wonder most of the signs one sees in public are so poor.

There is much boastful talk about the allegedly high state of typographic design in our time. One can, however, only deplore it. There are, to be sure, some outstanding lettering artists among us, but these are the exception, and they have little influence on the use to which letters are put. The craft of sign painters and designers still depends on the pallid reworkings of once beautiful classical alphabets. Or it depends on the already weakened or even immature elaborations on these originals. Rarely are sign painters, graphic artists and typographers led to the genuine sources of the art of lettering.

These sources are the classic expression of our basic letter forms which are unknown to most. It is essential to know them and to be guided by them. Letters evolved historically. They must be studied to be mastered. No one can invent letters by himself. At best we can modify them. But only those who have mastered the best of the older letter forms are entitled to modify them. This easily takes half of a lifetime. It is far better to keep one's hands off and not be lead astray by the false notion that lettering calls for 'self expression'. This error is largely responsible for the ugly lettering which surrounds us. Even some acknowledged masters among recent lettering artists have succumbed to this error to a regrettable extent. The essence of good lettering is precisely the opposite of what, until recently, has been widely preached: it is not self-expression, but complete self-negation in the service of a correctly understood task. What good is it if a sign painter, who has learned only a highly personal style of broad pen lettering, puts this already distorted form of lettering on a building whose architectural style is not compatible? Even if the lettering style happens to be good, the result will be bad. The all important point that the letter style must be appropriate to the use to which it is put, has not been considered. There can be exceptions, of course. But not every letter style, not even every good one, can be used anywhere without respect for the architecture. Before applying a letter, we must, therefore, apply good taste.

Taste, good taste, can only be developed by studying the best examples. No one is born with good taste; it is always the result of education. The inexperienced do not have it. If the letters surrounding us were good, good letters might set a trend. But since even poor design so often becomes fashionable, and since almost all lettering is bad, no improvement is in sight unless some good designers set a good example. If this occurred, there would soon be imitators.

The lettering student must first of all forget all the letter forms that have been held up to him. He must acquaint himself with the correct, perfect, classic letters and thoroughly study them. This cannot be done quickly. Art takes time, and those who wish for quick results had better not start. Good lettering is, as a rule, created slowly. Only the master can, on occasion, work quickly; that is what makes him a master. Lettering, like all art, is not for the impatient.

This book, based on a lifetime of study, contains a careful selection of the best letters of our civilization up to the present. With the exception of a few, they will be unknown to many readers. Not all of them are to be used as models, for some of them can rarely, if ever, be applied. These examples demonstrate the development of our letters and should inspire a feeling for their beauty of form, character, lines, and arrangement. To study them will not harm the novice; a master, however, will approach them with greater understanding. At least half of the letters shown can be copied directly and it is up to each reader and his purposes to select the one with which he wishes to begin.

At first one must master *one* letter form. Some readers will strive to become specialists of, say, an oldstyle letter (pages 84 to 87), a sans serif (page 202), or a Bodoni (page 174 and 175). If *one* letter form is properly understood, it is easier to grasp others. They are models to be literally and studiously copied. Teachers of lettering in recent years have shied away from supplying such models and denied that their own letters should also be imitated. The erroneous cult of 'self expression' did not permit them to furnish valid models to others.

This, however, *is* a source book, providing examples of the highest order and, at times, ultimate perfection. 'Do likewise!' reads an inscription on the Berne

Cathedral. You cannot do better. Leave everything else behind you. Not the bad, not the mediocre, only perfection is worth copying. Devote yourself willingly to the study of the most noble letter forms. You will not only earn recognition, but your city will also some day bear the stamp of your skill.

Many signs and inscriptions have a long life. This prospect demands that each character be carefully shaped. To rush the design of an inscription which will presumably be seen for ten or twenty years is wrong. If it is to be really good, a thorough study of the architecture, of the buildings around it and, usually, several careful preliminary drawings are necessary. Only architectural letters, letters that are drawn, are suitable for this purpose, not those that are spontaneously written with a flat brush, like cardboard signs at a county fair. Good lettering, just as good carpentry work, is not a matter of minutes.

Three emblems designed by the author. Left: Colophon for a publisher. Center: Signet for *Typographische Monatsblätter*, Sankt Gallen, Switzerland, with the two letters t and m as a typesetter sees them. Right: Private monogram, E.T.

GOOD AND BAD LETTERS

WHEN the Austrian reformer of lettering, Rudolf von Larisch set out, some fifty years ago, to reform the decadent lettering of his time, he taught that letter forms should not be based on tradition. Lettering men, he said, should develop their own imagination and create beautiful forms of their own. It turned out that this thesis is just barely sufficient for the design of sans-serif letters, but that it fails if roman and blackletter styles are to be well designed. As early as 1910 Larisch published a portfolio of reproductions of very beautiful calligraphic letters of past centuries and his book, *Lessons in Ornamental Lettering,* which first appeared in 1905, it is true, also contains a large reproduction of an ancient Roman inscription. Nevertheless, no one really believed in providing models in those days and the source books of the time were not really suitable for any practical purpose. Larisch and his contemporaries made a personal style the aim of teaching lettering. This ideal has lost much of its former luster. Today even the best lettering of the period between 1908 and 1920 is obsolete. The classic letter forms, on the other hand, have remained young and full of vitality.

A personal letter form of any period differs from the classic form on which it is always based only because of its modifications, and seldom do these modifications stand comparison with the original. Almost inevitably they are only coarse distortions.

It happens rarely that an artist adds a new and equally good letter form to the best ones of the past. If he is wise, he will not even attempt to do so but instead will select some of the classic letter forms as his model. If he strives to apply these forms in the spirit of their creators and their time, he will sooner or later get a better feeling for letter forms than if he bothers with mediocre and half-understood styles.

Some good letters of unique, personal design were, of course, also created in our time. But it is dilettantism to repeat them. Like the creators of these good, personal contemporary letter forms, everyone who draws or paints letters should turn directly to the best historical sources and study them thoroughly. This is not only the most sensible course, but is also the only way to become a master of lettering with a personal expression, assuming that this is a desirable ideal. Perfection cannot be improved but only imitated.

Lettering performs a service; it must be legible. A letter which we cannot read is useless, one which we can read only with difficulty is poor, and only a letter that is legible fulfills its proper function. But a legible letter still is not necessarily beautiful. Just as we like to surround ourselves with beautiful objects, we consciously or unconsciously enjoy beautiful and noble letter forms. It is the task of all those who work with alphabets to enhance our environment with beautiful lettering. Letters should not be merely a necessary evil which daily offends our eyes. They should not only serve but also delight. This requires a clear, consistent, perfect letter in excellent, well balanced applications.

A functional and beautiful letter conveys the symbols of the alphabet in harmonious form which does not suppress any of its distinct characteristics. Every lettering style is subject to its own prescribed law, its own definite form. The unique shape of the 52 capitals and lower case letters may, however, not be violated for the sake of mere decoration. The recurring details in each of the alphabet symbols must be the same or related and their relative width must be consistent. There are no set rules for the relative proportion of height and width of a letter. It is somewhat

Specimens from a horror chamber of contemporary lettering:
Logotypes that failed.

Englebert: Swollen, tortured lower case letters. Unnatural connection between E and t. Ugly g, such as a pretentious, uncultured person might write it. The crossbar of t is too high. Very poor.

Vespa: No feeling for form. The letters are incredibly bad. The insipid line under the word is of no help. Graphologists say that underlining of one's own name means either that the writer fears not to be taken seriously or that he wants to show off.

Armstrong: This A, bad enough as it is, does not lend itself to this kind of elongated stroke. Outmoded, rhythmically poor letters.

Richard: One of many examples of the foolish desire to connect the first and last letters of a name by means of a contrived line that is meant to be "organic." In this case it is the D which is rendered almost illegible as a result.

?aub: Should be read as "Laub." Very poor Fraktur letters. The L is unclear because the main stroke has been misused to support the rest of the letters. The b is ill conceived and topheavy. The upper strokes of the u and the end strokes of the a and u are too long.

Pirelli: The main part of the P is so absurdly elongated that the word becomes incomprehensible.

??ahmann: This should read "W. Rahmann." The tail of the R is stiff and too heavy at the end. W and R cannot be merged like this, since the W becomes most unclear. The curve of the R is much too large and seems forced. The lower case letters are mediocre.

Canadad: Should read "Candida." But the first d looks like an a because of its crippled ascender. The white i-dot on the loop is a mistake. Although the C is not good, its beginning flourish is genuine. The tail end of the a is too forced. It is a poor attempt at symmetrical design. Symmetrical word images are particularly hard to read.

Hoover: The crossbar of the H is too low so that the H is not readily recognized. No one, not even a person who writes an H like this, would draw out the crossbar that far to load it with the rest of the letters. These lower case letters are typical of the bloated stiffness of "modern" logotypes.

different for each letter style. Only very rarely can it be expressed in a simple numerical proportion, and even then only by chance. It has always been the human eye, and an extremely sensitive eye at that, which has given certain letter styles their definite and enduring proportion. Compass and ruler are good accessory tools, but they do not create form. Time and again there have been attempts to freeze letter forms into some relatively simple numerical ratio or a geometric construction of the compass. This, however, has only succeeded when the designer had the desired letter form already in his mind's eye. Attempts at construction have usually failed because such a vision was lacking. Even the famous constructed Renaissance roman letters, like those of Luca Pacioli (1509) and of Albrecht Dürer (1525), which are so often cited, are in no way the best models. They are, it should at last be said, quite overrated and therefore have not been included in this book. Later attempts of this kind were successfully done only by truly accomplished lettering masters.

The desirable harmony of a letter, it seems, can only be created and perceived

RIMO KRIMO FIAT PIRAS

BUSCH KNOPF ENGLEBERT

Examples of poor sans serif capitals.

Rimo: Much too condensed, with the result that the M is absurdly distorted and the R is unclear. Very condensed letters must be opened up with liberal letter spacing; otherwise they become completely illegible.

Krimo: There are three frequent mistakes here. The K cannot be designed like this. Its arms must branch out from one point (see page 205). The head of the R is too large. It should come in at the middle of the vertical, not below it. The correct form is shown on page 205. The M is very poor. The two proper alternatives are shown on page 205. The rhythm of the entire word image is faulty. The spacing between K and R should be carried through. The letters are somewhat too heavy. An O which is drawn with a compass makes the horizontal portions optically too thick.

Firt: Does not mean Firt but Fiat. The A is very poor. The horizontal strokes of F and T are optically too thick.

Piras: Much too heavy. There is no reason for such bold letters. The swollen heads of P and R are the result of exaggeratedly thick lines. The S is clumsy; the upper and lower loops should not deteriorate into horizontals. The whole word is ugly but, unfortunately, rather typical.

Busch: Generally much too heavy. Hence the dark B which is also too wide. The endings of S and C would be better cut perpendicularly as shown in page 204. Horizontal stroke of H is too heavy.

Knopf: The same mistake as in *Piras;* everything is much too heavy. Very poor form of the K, even worse than the K in *Krimo* above. The proper form of K is shown on page 204.

Englebert: In this word only the first E is correct. The two other E's are poor because they do not look like the first. The N is too pointed and too small. The G has an inappropriate thorn. The loops of G, B and R are too angular and their corners are too thick. The swollen head of the R is ludicrous. The crossbar of the T is too heavy. Poor rhythm; only the spacing between L and E and between R and T is correct; all the other letters are too close together.

by the eye and not by the brain. The supreme rule is that no letter may be allowed to become conspicuous in the company of others. If one letter stands out, it is poorly designed. An O which is too large is just as deficient as one that is too small. A letter that is too strong must be given the right thickness of lines. If a g stands out, its form is wrong. All these faults are grave errors that need no elaboration. A good alphabet is like a harmonious group of people in which no one misbehaves.

Even ordinary lettering requires uniformity and harmony in all its details. But such lettering is still far from being beautiful. Our efforts must thus be directed towards the very best and most beautiful form.

Good letters consist of more than a composition of lines. Not everyone recognizes the importance of the inner forms, the shape of the negative white spaces within the letter. A perfect letter always shows beautiful inner spaces. These must be as uncluttered, simple and noble as the movement and silhouette of the black shapes. Lack of attention to this inner form often makes the entire letter unsatisfactory.

Rheinbrücke Koller
Möbel Hubacher corrodi

Examples of poor sans serif lower case letters.

Rheinbrücke: These letters have been "invented" with ruler and compass and therefore appear unnatural. The e is too wide, the R much too narrow. The ascenders seem emaciated, the i dots glued on. The k is extremely poor. All horizontal lines appear heavier than the verticals. There is no rhythm whatsoever; the letters are stuck together and their openings look like holes.

Koller: It is not possible to use a wedge shape for the vertical lines of ll because this form cannot be adapted to our letters. Consider the o and e: there is nothing wedge-shaped here. The K is much too small. The r is much too large and there is no connection between the circle and the basic stroke. Such an r is impossible. The crossbar of the e is also much too low.

Möbel Hubacher: The M and the H are much too large and the M is too light in relation to the H. The dots over the ö are much too high. The lower case letters might pass but they are too tightly spaced.

corrodi: The d is too long, even though we can appreciate the attempt to emphasize the contour of the word image. The slanted line over the i is not an i dot but looks like an accent mark. Only a dot is really legible. The ends of c and r do not harmonize. The ends of the c are not heavy enough and the circles of the r's appear too thick and might be lightened by a vertical white line like the other verticals.

Nor is it the well balanced relationship of the widths of the various lower case letters alone that determines the good quality of lettering. The suitable length of ascenders and descenders in relation to the height of the n, and the size and line strength of the capital letters are equally important.

The ascenders and descenders of a letter style create the characteristic word image. They determine legibility. If the ascenders and descenders are too short, the word image becomes indistinct. We should, therefore, shun such exaggerations. A beautiful letter must be clear and intelligible. Intelligibility suffers if the ascenders and decenders are too short. There is no rule for the 'correct' relative height of an h and a p to the height of an n. It differs a little in all letter styles. Nor can it always be expressed in such a simple ratio as 1:1 or 2:3. Theories about this are nonsense. The 'correct' height of an h is partly determined by the relative thickness of the lines of the letter and other characteristics of each letter style. The descenders, however, should never be shorter than the ascenders. This is all too often forgotten, as is shown by the example on page 37.

Finally we have to consider the size of the capital letter in relation to that of the lower case letter. Originally, lower case letters stood by themselves. Their forms derive from the penned Carolingian minuscule (page 58 and 59). The upper and lower case letters received their present form in the Renaissance. The serifs of the capitals, or upper case letters, were adapted to those of the lower case alphabet. The capitals are based on an incised or chiseled letter; the lower case characters are based on a pen-written calligraphic form. Now the two kinds of letters appear together. But the original difference is still evident in our roman alphabets. There is no genuine relationship between the height of the ascenders and the height of the capitals; they actually have nothing to do with each other. The fact that the two kinds of letters are equally high in most letter styles does not mean that they must be so. Let us also consider that most ascenders only form a peak while most capitals are topped by a broad plane. To appear as prominent as an E or a B, the peak must be slightly higher. This becomes difficult in the later roman letters, such as those of Bodoni, for example (pages 174 and 175). Since here the serifs are horizontal, the eye seeks a visible relation to the height of the capital letter. In the old style roman letters, such as that of Aldus Manutius, which today is called Bembo (125), or the Centaur (124), it is far easier to determine an appropriate proportion between upper and lower case. In these typefaces the upper serifs of the ascenders are slanted, and this harmonizes far better with moderate size capitals. It is much better if the capitals are not quite as high as the ascenders of the lower case characters. Capitals which are as high as the top of the lower case ascenders often seem conspicuous. Their weight seems unbalanced in relation to that of the lower case

Interlaken Arosa

Left: Lettering which tries to appear fresh and spontaneous but actually looks heavy, distorted, and stiff. The I and t are poor and the k is out of proportion. None of the letters are good. All are forced and cramped.
Right: Example of a rather good solution of a similar problem. The spontaneity of the original sketch has survived. One feels the retouching, however. Retouching is necessary but it should not be apparent.

Examples of excellent free brush lettering (reduced from original size).
Left above: Lines from an American advertisement. Letters show unusual right slant of the edge of the brush.
Left below: From an American advertisement. The freshness of the first, casual sketch has been retained.
Right: Title page of a Chinese book on seals. 1943. Excellent example of Chinese calligraphy. No corrections can be made on Chinese paper. Every line must be perfect or the calligrapher has to start over again. The square seal on the bottom left is bright vermilion red.

letters that follow them. On page 126 is the most beautiful Renaissance Roman I know. But most people will rightly consider the capitals of this typeface a little too large and prominent. For example, look at the word Bible in the second line. The l is actually exactly as tall as the B but seems to be shorter. The B should be shorter so that the l would appear to be just as tall. All the capitals on the page are, furthermore, too heavy. Capitals are, of course, always a little heavier than lower case letters and should be. But one discovers this only on measuring them; it should not be evident. If the letters on page 126 are used, the size of the capitals should be slightly reduced. This will also reduce the strength of the strokes and give them the proper weight.

The letterer deals not only with capital and lower case letters but also with numerals. These seem to be the stepchildren of letter design. We need only look at our house numbers. Many people believe that numerals must be of equal height because that is what they learned in school. However, this is not the case. Legible numerals are not equally high but have ascenders and descenders just like lower case letters. Of course, sometimes the use of numerals of equal height is appropriate, such as in a line of capitals, but these occasions are rare. An ascending or descending numeral is not only more beautiful but also more legible if used together with the older lower case forms. Those who love letters will do well to note beautiful old letter forms on buildings or elsewhere and to include them in their collections of type specimens. The numerals that give the dates of old houses are often marvelous. They delight the eye because their image is often as well articulated as a word of lower case letters, to say nothing of the form of the numerals themselves. Figures also provide a welcome ornament.

290 1675 384 Mm

Oldstyle numerals (Garamond).
They have ascenders and descenders, and are more legible than numerals of equal height.

290 1675 384 Mm

Modern numerals (Bodoni). All are the same height and thus less intelligible.

Numerals originally belonged to neither lower case nor capitals. They derive from a different culture as they are based on Arabic forms. This is the reason that they always appear a bit strange. If numerals are shown along with letters, they must be of the same style. Their form elements, however, have little in common with those of the letters. It is up to the letterer to make these contradictions unnoticeable.

What has been said so far points to the important characteristics of well formed letters, but does not define just what determines their beauty. Only penetrating study and practice can teach the difference between mediocre or even poor letters and beautiful ones. There is no limit to the amount of study one can give to the models in this book. The slightest detail of any of the letters should not be overlooked. The beginner should not think that he will recognize the full beauty of these examples right away. Only after long study and practice in copying does one grasp the vital importance of each detail and of the specific shape of a letter in relation to its entire alphabet. Here or there one may think that a minor change is desirable. But respect for the traditional forms and a real feeling for them (which comes with experience) demand that even the slightest variations be made with caution.

THE OLDER LETTER FORMS

THE history of our alphabet begins with the letters of the ancient Romans. They are the letters used at the time of Cicero and Caesar. The Romans, however, did not invent their letters. They took over the Greek alphabet as used by Greek colonists in Southern Italy, replacing some unsuitable characters with others. Some Greek characters were adapted to symbolize different Roman sounds.

The Roman letters reached their highest perfection at the end of the first century after Christ after an evolution of about a hundred years. The most beautiful example is the inscription on the Trajan column in Rome (pages 50 to 53). These letters, called *capitalis romana,* which are on the average 4 inches high, were painted on the stone with a flat brush and then incised with a chisel. The soft swelling of the curves are the result of the brush used like a pen. The well articulated endings of the letters owe their form to the artist's intention to decisively finish the line on the top and on the bottom. The proportions of this justly acclaimed alphabet are of great nobility and have rarely, if ever, been surpassed. The Trajan column lettering continues to be the source from which all our type styles derive.

For their books the Romans used a reed pen cut to form a broad edge. They developed two letter forms, a slow and a fast one. The slow letter is called *quadrata* (page 54a and b). One of its variations (54a) was written with a pen which had a straight-cut edge held almost parallel to the base line of the letter. Another variation shows a more slanted position of the pen (54b), that is, the edge was cut to be held at an angle to the base line. The *rustica* (54c), written with a pen cut at an even steeper angle, could be written faster. Quadrata and rustica are the formal book letters of the ancient Romans. The writing they used for correspondence was done with a stylus on wax tablets or with a very narrow reed pen on papyrus. It was the *early Roman cursive.* Roman inscriptions and Roman book letters are of equal height. In the early Roman cursive, however, several parts of the letter protrude beyond the upper and lower lines. This handwriting is the forerunner of a new letter style, the *uncial* (55b, 55c, 56a, 60). The uncial not only shows several ascenders and descenders, but also rather frequent curves which replace formerly straight lines. E, D, H, M are now round. L, D, H have ascenders, P and Q descenders. The uncial has variations of upright (55b, 56a, 60) and slanted pen positions (55c). The later Roman period used a *later Roman cursive* (56b) for its handwriting. Its forms are similar to those of the uncial. Ascenders and descenders are used as a means to increase legibility. These are even more distinct in the *half uncial* (56c). The characters d, b, f and a resemble our lower case letters. A particularly beautiful half uncial was used in Ireland and England; the Book of Kells (57) is the most magnificent example. This gospel book shows slow letters of great perfection.

The most important event in the history of Western letters was the formation of the *Carolingian minuscule* (58, 59, 61, 62). It was the thoughtful creation of Bishop Alcuin of York, whom Charlemagne called to his court, to take charge of educating his people. The Carolingian minuscule is the first genuine minuscule or lower case letter, and closely resembles our lower case characters. The lower case t still does not have a peak, but the n, one of the most important letters, has already found its modern form. These letters were written rather speedily with a very broad pen held at an angle to the base line.

It was not only the change in the style of the period which slowly broke the round forms of the Carolingian minuscule. There was also a quest for knowledge on the part of the priests, the only ones at the time who could read and write, and they demanded more and more theological literature. Lettering became more hasty, compressed and angular. Finally, angularity and compression were elevated to a style principle. The result was the *blackletter*. The pointed, angular blackletter, also called *Textura* (64, 65, 67, 73), used in the north of Europe, is distinguished from *round Gothic* or *Rotunda* (63, 72) which still shows some curves, has not completely departed from the Carolingian minuscule, and was used primarily in Italy and Spain.

At the end of the Middle Ages a new letter style emerged which was a conscious copy of the Carolingian letters. With the exception of the dot over the i which now appeared, the calligraphy of the early Italian Renaissance often can hardly be distinguished from that of the Carolingian period. The new letters, however, soon assumed somewhat independent form (74, 75, 78). Today's roman typefaces are based on it since it served the early printers as a model (76). This written *Humanistic minuscule,* or *lettera antica,* was a book letter. The handwriting of the Italian Renaissance, the *Humanistic cursive,* which was soon known as *Cancellaresca* (79, 80, 81), could be written faster, and was really new. It served as a model for our *italic* typefaces, the sister of roman.

As yet the art of lettering was in the hands of papal or court scribes. But meanwhile printing had been invented and took over all book making. The calligrapher was left to apply his art to penning contracts and to teaching.

Two basic categories of type styles have been in use since Gutenberg's invention: the roman and the blackletter.

roman blackletter

Roman letters fall into two groups: (1) Letters with varying thick and thin lines, and (2) Letters with lines of even thickness – sans serif and Egyptian.

Roman Sans serif Egyptian

The roman letters with varying thick and thin lines divide into four groups: (1) Venetian, (2) Oldstyle, (3) Transitional, and (4) Modern.

The Venetian typefaces rely on the written Humanistic Minuscule, the Italian book letter of the early Renaissance (74, 75). The version cut in 1470 by Nicolaus Jenson (page 76) is the most beautiful. But Venetian, by and large, does not differ much from the slightly later oldstyle. Its most distinct feature is the crossline of the e; another distinction is that the upper serifs of the M also continue inwards. The typeface designed by the American typographer Bruce Rogers (124) is based on Jenson's face.

The oldstyle also derives from the written form (Bembo, 125, de Tournes, 126; Garamond, 128). Here, however, the crossbar of the e is horizontal and the capitals reveal a careful study of the ancient Roman inscriptions. The upper serifs of the l, b, d and i, j, m, n, u are slanted as in the calligraphic letters. The slanted swelling of the curves is also based on the calligraphic forms. The top and bottom serifs of the capital letters are slightly rounded towards the vertical lines.

Oldstyle, lbdijmoeft

Oldstyle letters were used from the Renaissance until the middle of the eighteenth century. The best known among them is the family of typefaces cut after the original Garamond. One of these is used for the text of this book. However, as was learned only after the Garamond typefaces had already been given their name, it is actually based on a typeface created in 1621 by the Swiss typecutter Jean Jannon of Sedan.

As time went on, the difference between thick and thin lines was increasingly emphasized. Letters became more pointed. This becomes evident in the noble and expressive typeface called after Anton Janson of Leipzig, about 1670. This type (140, 141) shows the Dutch style of the late seventeenth century, which served as a basis for the type of the English typecutter William Caslon (144 to 147). Caslon did not attain the full beauty of its model, but it has proven its usefulness over more than two centuries.

The forms of the transitional style are exactly between oldstyle and modern. The upper serifs of the l, b, d and i, j, m, n, u which, in oldstyle, are set at an angle of 45 degrees, are now less slanted. The curves swell almost horizontally and thicken

Schematic demonstration of the primary distinction between
oldstyle, transitional roman and modern.

more suddenly than in oldstyle typefaces. The swellings are, however, still curved on the inside. The influence of the copper engravers of the eighteenth century can be felt. The transitional group includes the roman typefaces of John Baskerville of 1751 (160–163) and John Bell's of 1788 (164, 165), as well as the letters of J. F. Rosart (157), J. P. Fournier the Younger (158, 159), Fry's Ornamented (166), and Old Face Open (167).

Modern typefaces, the most famous of which was designed by Giambattista Bodoni in 1790, cancel all memories of the original calligraphic form (172–175). All serifs are horizontal and extremely thin, contrasting without transitional inner curves with the thick verticals. Even such details as the crossbars of the f and t, which are so important to legibility, are as thin as the serifs. Only the italic retains some calligraphic features, but even here the principle of geometric construction is carried as far as possible. The swelling of the curves is exactly vertical and occurs,

Modern, lbdijmoeft

so to speak, abruptly. The inner side of these curves is straight. Neither Didot (176, 177, and 171) nor the German typeface Walbaum (180, 181), both contemporaries of Bodoni, went quite as far as he did in carrying out this concept of the period.

The ultra-bold modern letter, first seen in 1807, has one of the most grotesque appearances in the history of letter design. It shows exaggeratedly thick basic strokes and the thinnest possible connecting lines (182, 183, 186, 187, 188, 195). The group of typefaces known today as sans serif (still often misleadingly called Gothic in English speaking countries) first appeared in 1832. It seemed so weird at first that the Germans called it 'Grotesque'.

Egyptian, known since about 1815, like sans serif, has lines of equal strength.

The distinctive feature of Egyptian is its serifs which are almost as thick as the basic strokes (190, 191, 193, 196). Two of its variations are the Italienne (197) and the Clarendon (199).

All roman letter forms since 1540, with the exception of the Egyptian, have a matching italic. This always relates to the upright letters but the a and e are always borrowed from the written form. Even Bodoni retained this. It is regrettable that

Oldstyle Italic, anefmpjt   *Modern Ital c, anefmpjt*

some recent modern italics show an a and e which are essentially of the same design as the roman *a* and *e* but slanted. Aside from its narrower and cursive character, it is particularly the typical form of the a and e which gives the italic alphabet its distinction. To do away with this difference defeats the purpose of italic letters.

The blackletter is divided in four groups: (1) Round Gothic or Rotunda, (2) Pointed blackletter, (3) Schwabacher, and (4) Fraktur.

The first three belong to the Gothic style; the *Fraktur* of 1513 (104–111) is a creation of the German Renaissance. The completely broken form, which Gutenberg also used for the Forty-Two Line Bible, should be called Pointed blackletter rather than Gothic (64). The Rotunda (72) was re-created in our time. Its best design originated with Emil Rudolf Weiss. The Schwabacher of about 1470, which had been long forgotten (102, 121), is occasionally used again in Germany.

The four blackletter categories are easily recognizable by their lower case characters. In the Textur, the North European letter of the late Gothic period, all curves of the lower case characters are broken. The Rotunda, used in Italy and Spain in the fifteenth century, does not go as far, but at least the upper endings of the n and related forms are broken. In the Schwabacher, which came out of the late Gothic text type in Germany, even the ɑ and ꝺ are rounded on both sides and all forms are more pointed than in the Rotunda. The ᵷ which is crossed at right is also

amꝺmomꝋmi	amꝺmomꝋmi
Pointed blackletter	Rotunda
amꝺmomꝋmi	amꝺmomꝋi
Schwabacher	Fraktur

characteristic and so is the ᷤ. In *Fraktur,* the German Renaissance letter, the letters which in the Schwabacher are round on both sides, are half round and half broken.

The best commonly used example of the old Fraktur is the Luther Fraktur of the seventeenth and eighteenth centuries (122). More recent beautiful forms are the Unger Fraktur of 1794 (178) and the Walbaum Fraktur of the early nineteenth century (179).

The second third of the nineteenth century produced a surprising number of highly imaginative and partly fantastic letter forms. Most of them are rarely seen today, though in their basic form they could well be used in architecture since over half of our buildings belong to the nineteenth century. In this book I can only show a small selection of the variety of these letter styles (pages 182–203).

Classification and Nomenclature of Basic Letter Forms

MAIN GROUPS

I. Letters of Latin Origin	{	A. Roman Letters
		B. Blackletters
II. Letters of Non-Latin Origin		Greek, Semitic, Arabic, Chinese, etc.

LETTERS OF LATIN ORIGIN

Roman	With varying thick and thin strokes	Slanted stress	*Venetian*	see page 76	1470 –1500*
			Oldstyle with Italic	eMgm*em*	1495 –1757
		Intermediate vertical stress	*Transitional with Italic*	eMgm *eMgm*	1757 –1790
		Straight vertical stress	*Modern with Italic*	eMgm*em*	1790*–1900*
	With strokes of equal strength	Without serifs	*Sans serif Sans serif Italic*	eMgm	since 1832
		With serifs	*Egyptian*	eMgm eMgm	since 1815*
Blackletter	Tops of **inm** are broken; curves as in Carolingian Minuscule with tendency of breaking but without sharp points		*Rotunda*	emosдаv	since 1486
	Almost all strokes of lower case letters are broken		*Pointed blackletter*	emosдаv	since 1455
	Both sides of **osдаv** are rounded, sharp points; characteristic **g** is crossed at right		*Schwabacher*	emosдаv	since 1470*
	osдаv are half round and half broken		*Fraktur*	emosдаv	since 1513*

(Gothic Period spans the Rotunda, Pointed blackletter, Schwabacher, and Fraktur rows.)

*approximately

THE USE OF CAPITALS

THE foremost rule for the letter spacing of capitals is to achieve a rhythmically perfect harmony of the word image or line. Letter spacing means the distribution of appropriate spaces between letters. A word of capital letters which is not letter spaced is always unsatisfactory. Unfortunately, however, the need to letter space lines of capitals, at least a little, is all too rarely recognized. Many people know that letters such as A, J, L, P, T, V and W tear holes into the line and therefore adjust words which contain these letters. But this is often done by reducing the length of the crossbar of the L or T or by otherwise modifying the shape of the letter.

Letters are immutable. The rhythmic word image may not be forced at the expense of the proper shape of its letters. If an L is followed by an A, a hole results which seems to pose an insoluble problem to many lettering men. The L cannot be shortened. The L and A cannot be pulled closer together. Both these statements indicate that capital letters cannot always stand close together. Keeping them too tight is, however, always wrong, even for a word like MEN or HIM which does not contain any open letters.

The first thing to realize is that the rhythm of a well formed word can never be based on equal linear distances between letters. Only the visual space between letters matters. This unmeasurable space must always be of equal size. But only the eye can measure it, not the ruler. The eye is the judge of all visual matter, not the brain. The most difficult task is the equal spacing of sans serifs. Here even the slightest faults are shown up. I have therefore chosen this letter style for the examples in this discussion. The rules below, however, apply not only to sans serifs but also to other roman letter styles.

Far too little attention has been given to the problem of letter spacing capitals. Rudolf von Larisch demanded that the distances between capitals be spatial and not, as towards the end of the nineteenth century, based on equal linear distances alone. This rule is not sufficient, however. There are not only letters like L and A but also other open letters like O which can be disturbing in many other ways. Since some people do not know how to handle a circular O, they believe it should not be circular. But it is not the circular O, the correct form in some letter styles, that is at fault, but the lettering man who has not given sufficient thought to making the circular O an inconspicuous part of the word image.

As long as the circular O is placed rather closely to other letters, its white inner circle cuts a perceivable hole into the line. If the neighboring letter is moved far enough away so that the white space surrounding the circumference of the O is optically equal to its inner opening, this hole disappears. I call this 'neutralizing'. The minimum spacing between capitals must always be equal to this optical value, even if the word image contains neither an O, nor an open letter such as L or V. People who observe this rule will have no difficulty in fitting even the troublesome sequence LA into a rhythmically spaced word image.

WOOLWORTH   WOOLWORTH

Identical spacing between letters
results in word images that lack rhytm.
The O's make a hole because the letters are
generally too close.

Letter spacing should not be mechanically
equal but must achieve equal optical space.
The letters must be separated
by even and adequate white areas.

The rule can also be expressed differently. We shall see in the discussion of lower case that in the word "nun" the six perpendicular lines must be spaced approximately evenly. If we take the word NUN we are faced with the same problem. Here, too, the six vertical lines should be about equidistant. If this is taken as a guide, we achieve – by a different way – the same rhythm gained by neutralizing the circular O.

NUN   NUN

Unsatisfactory. Too close.   Satisfactory.

This rule covers the normal rhythm of letter spacing words in capital letters. They should never be spaced more tightly if flawless, beautiful lettering is to result. But they may be spaced more widely, even considerably more, particularly on buildings and shop fronts. Overly wide spacing at times may interfere with easy comprehension of the word image, even if the letters themselves are perfectly legible. The lettering may then appear like a string of pearls. This is not always a disadvantage as it may give the building an attractive decoration.

When we examine lower case letters, we will find that our eye skims along their upper line and that we actually read only their upper half. However, capitals are usually read as complete symbols. And yet the upper half is more important even for capitals than the lower half. This becomes evident if we compare the correct distance of an A to its neighboring letters with the distance of the equally wide V to its neighbors. The exact same distance seems too small, because the V spreads at the top.

A similar situation prevails when the correct distance to a T must be determined. Even if the space between T and the next letter is the same as between letters like H and E, the space must be increased slightly because of the T's crossbar.

THEO   THEO

The space between T and H is insufficient;
optically the crossbar of the T seems to hit the H.

Here this fault is removed. The space
between T and H has been slightly enlarged.

Even the L and A should never be put very close together. A certain amount of space between them is necessary. Otherwise the two letters look as though they are glued together. They must, however, be sufficiently separated if the effect is to be attractive.

PLANE   PLANE

There should always be a slight gap even between L and A. Otherwise these two letters seem glued together.

Here the distance between L and A is correct. The identity of each letter is now apparent.

As a general rule, if capitals are to achieve their full beauty, they should never be entangled without letter spacing even if there are no open letters. The word HUNDRED does not contain any particularly open letters. If it is spaced too closely the second vertical of the H and the first vertical of the U seem much too close, while both, in fact, all letters, seem to show their inner space rather than their actual outline. Such words are hard to read and lack beauty. Only if the distance between H and D is somewhat like the distance between the two vertical lines of the H, does the word become legible and beautiful. The seemingly undesirable openings on the right side of the R and E are now neutralized and seem natural. The letters can breathe. Capitals that are not letter spaced form a hard-to-read thicket.

HUNDRED HUNDRED

Unsatisfactory. A thicket of letters. Frequent mistake.

Legible, and attractive.

Word Spacing of Capitals

Harmonious spacing between words is just as important as correct letter spacing. Word spaces should be neither too wide nor too narrow. The best rule is to make the distance between words as wide as the letter I including the letter spacing that belongs to it. The frequently advocated rule of squeezing the width of an O between words is ill conceived as it does not take letter spacing into consideration. If the letters are widely spaced, a larger word space is required than if they were normally spaced. In designing fairly long lines which stand by themselves for building fronts, the word spacing may be increased a little so as to clearly keep the words apart. Yet the integrity of the line as a whole must be maintained. It should not be allowed to fall apart into single words.

MODERN DESIGN

The word spacing in a line of capitals should correspond to the width of an I plus the letter spacing used for the other letters in that line.

Punctuation within capital lines should be mentioned here. Periods and commas are undesirable. Occasionally, if correct spelling demands it, a hyphen is unavoidable. Periods are not used on inscriptions. Sometimes periods are asked for to denote abbreviations such as after the letters LTD although here, as well as in the abbreviation CO., they are not really necessary and should be avoided. However, there are other abbreviations for which a period cannot be omitted. It should then be placed on the base line and should not be too small or too large. Most important of all, the proper distance from the preceding letter must be found; as a rule, the period should not be glued to it. While the distance should not be as great as the normal letter space, tight spacing is wrong.

One way to indicate a separation of words in capital lines is to place a period above the base line at the height of the H crossbar. This symbol might have the size and form of the normal period in its letter style or in incised lettering, it may take the form of a small triangle.

PAINTS·WALLPAPER

Some lettering men use a slash of the height of the capital instead of this symbol. Such a slash is not only too long but also incorrect. It does not belong in capital lines but to blackletters. Slashes were used in Schwabacher and Fraktur which featured diagonal lines as high as the letters instead of commas (see pages 105, 106, 108, 121, 122). But slashes have no place in capital lines.

Line Spacing of Capitals

Capital letters have two guide lines, the lower one being the base line. The distance between two or more capital lines of the same height is determined by the layout. It is, nevertheless, useful to point out that the letter height and the space between

DEPARTMENT OF
THE INTERIOR

The word spaces seem like holes because of the narrow line spacing.

DEPARTMENT OF
THE INTERIOR

With adequate line spacing, the two lines seem uncluttered and attractive.

lines, like everything in lettering, represents a proportion. And perceptible proportion can be beautiful or ugly. If the total arrangement of the sign requires wide spacing between the lines, this proportion is no longer discernable. If the lines follow each other closely, good or bad proportion becomes apparent.

An excellent proportion is 1 to 1, that is, the distance between lines equals the height of the letters. The space between two lines of capitals should not be less than the letter height. Another possibility is the proportion 2 to 3; the distance between lines is one half larger than the letter height. Another good proportion is 1 to 2. This means the line spacing is exactly twice the height of the letter (as on the title page of this book).

The word spacing looks right only if the line spacing is not less than the letter height. If the line spacing is less than the letter height, the spaces between words look like holes and the entire composition becomes indistinct and ugly.

IT is generally assumed that it is simple to put lower case letters together. This overlooks the fact that lower case letters also have some open characters (k, r, t, v, w, x, y, z) and that they, too, contain the o which so often makes a hole in the line. Furthermore, we are too conditioned by the low level of lettering that surrounds us to be aware of the faults of most lower case word images, even the printed ones.

If one takes the trouble to investigate why today's lettering does not look as well as the most perfect of past lettering specimens, he will find that the past used a different rhythm. The lower case letters were not as crowded together as they are today.

forma virgultum brachium

forma virgultum brachium

The upper line shows some words of the specimen of Claude Garamond's types published in 1592. The lower line shows a modern Garamond. Note the perfect rhythm of the genuine Garamond. The later letters are too close together causing gaps after r and v, and generally lack the evenness of the older form. The rhythm and form of the original make it incomparably superior to the modern one.

The old lettering masters followed the rule that all the basic strokes of a word should be spaced at approximately equal distance. This rule is disregarded today; lower case letters are pushed together. This is why much lettering and even the better typefaces look deficient. The old rule, however, is still valid. Only if it is observed will the letters k, r, t, v, w, x, y, and z cease to create gaps in the word image, and the letters b, d, o, p and q cease to make holes.

mimi   **mimi**

Somewhat too tight.   Rhythmically correct.

unworthy   unworthy

Too close. The w makes holes.   Correct. Rhythmically perfect.

We learned that, if the architecture calls for it, capital letters may be letter spaced more widely than the rule demands. This is not true of lower case letters. There should be no letter spacing of lower case letters. They should be arranged only in their normal fitting. This prohibition is based on the fact that lower case letters have a more irregular outline than capital letters. In addition to characters of the normal height of n, there are also letters with ascenders (b, d, f, h, k, l) and descenders (g, j, p, q, y), and the t which has a short point on top. This gives the word image

unworthy   u n w o r t h y

Satisfactory.   Unsatisfactory.

The left word shows the correct rhythm of lower case letters. The word at right is letter spaced hence difficult to read. In single lines letter spacing of lower case letters is questionable; if more than one line is involved, letter spacing of lower case letters is wrong.

of lower case letters a characteristic form which the words of capitals lack. Capitals always form a square, only rarely enlivened by the tail of a Q or an accent. The characteristic form of the lower case words makes them far easier to perceive than words lettered in capitals. Nevertheless, lower case words are rarely suitable on buildings. What matters here is not the speed of comprehension but the harmony of the façade. This, by its very nature, calls for architectural letters rather than those which derive from calligraphy as the lower case letters do.

Lower case letters were originally a calligraphic form, written with a pen. Since this form has long been fixed and is unchangeable, attempts to change the calligraphic character in favor of a constructed one will never succeed. Take a look at

nhmurpq nhmurpq

the n and m. It is easy to see how the arch leading to the second vertical stroke of the n starts, as written with a broad pen, a little under the upper line of the letter. That is why the forms of the n, h, m, u, r, p and q are never quite satisfactory in sans serif letters. In roman alphabets the beginning and endings of these letters are thin because the upward stroke of the broad pen made them so. In sans serifs they must be thick. This leads to thickenings which only masters can make relatively inconspicuous.

Lower case letters are suitable only for independent signs and longer texts. There they are welcome so that the content can be quickly grasped. Lower case words impress the mind with their total silhouette while capitals are mentally spelled out letter by letter.

But it is not only the silhouette we read. It can easily be proven that the eye grasps the upper half of the word image. It is far more important than the lower half. The following example shows that we cannot easily decipher the lower half of a word if we cover the upper half. But we can read the upper half relatively well if the lower half is cut away. This furnishes a good test for the relative legibility of roman and sans serif letters. What we read are the characteristic features of a letter, not what all the characters of the alphabet have in common. That is why a good letter must clearly show its distinguishing features.

quer auer galapagos   quer auer galapagos

quer auer galapagos

A beautiful letter must naturally have unity of form. It must, for instance, have the same thickness of the basic strokes, of serifs, of related curves, and so forth. But if the number of these form elements is excessively reduced, as happens when the characteristic features are suppressed, legibility is threatened. The a and g of some sans serifs and Egyptians, which, in the manner of the italics of type styles that have serifs (a and g), are designed as ɑ and g, reduce the legibility of the word image. They are falsely considered up-to-date. Viewed by themselves they may seem "simpler" than the forms a and g, but that is not the point. The primary purpose of a letter is not simplicity but legibility. And ɑ and g are less intelligible. The

quer auer galapagos   quer auer galapagos

quer auer galapagos   quer auer galapagos

upper half of ɑ and g are identical and, furthermore, the same as that of q. We thus have three letters with the same upper half. No two characters of the roman alphabet have an upper half of the same shape, which is what makes them legible. If there are suddenly three different, important characters with the same upper half, the word images are bound to become more blurred than normal word images whose upper halves are distinct and different. The use of ɑ and g in sans serif, roman or Egyptian letters is, therefore, a poor innovation. This can be demonstrated with several words. Long texts of sans serifs are hard to read, at any rate, and the lack of distinction of the seemingly "modern" ɑ and g increases this difficulty.

Sans Serif and Egyptian letters with the ɑ and g seem more decorative than the same letters with a correct a and g, because they contain more circular openings. The frequent repetition of the circular element makes a line of these letters more decorative than that of other faces. But the decorative value is achieved at the expense of readability, just as the Textur with its distinct fracture of all details, results in a band of lettering that is highly decorative but hard to read. I therefore prefer the sans serif ɑ and g designed by Eric Gill (204, 205) which derives from the classic form of the oldstyle. Gill's emulation of oldstyle forms is also evident in his improved articulation of the characters b, j, s, t, u and J, Q, R, S, and G. The capitals are borrowed from the Roman inscriptions (49–53) and the endings of C, G, J and S are uniform as in the Roman letters.

Word Spacing in Lower Case Lines

Word spacing in lower case lines is more often too large rather than too small. Since the lower case letters do not feature openings as large as those in capitals, the word spacing should also be relatively smaller. In lines of lower case characters of average width, the measurable distance between two words should be about

Old and New   Old and New

Unsatisfactory.   Satisfactory.

twice as wide as a third of the height of the n. An o at the beginning of a word demands a somewhat smaller word space than n. In all of this, it is the optical space value that matters.

In condensed letters the word spacing may even be smaller. In very extended letters it should be a little larger.

Line Spacing of Lower Case Letters

Lower case letters have four guide lines. The space between two inner ones is called the n height. The line on which the n rests is called the base line. The uppermost guide line determines the limit of the ascenders (though not necessarily the upper limit of the capital); the lowest line determines the lowest point of the descenders. Well formed descenders contribute as much to legibility as the ascenders. In some recent letters these descenders are inappropriately shortened. They seem weak, timid, and unclear.

allegory   allegory

Descenders of correct length.   Stunted descenders.

The smallest line spacing is that in which the descenders of the upper line touch the ascenders of the line below. The danger of this actually occuring is small. However, such close line spacing is rarely in order.

If the previously stated rule regarding word spacing is followed, word spacing will be considerably smaller than line spacing. This is necessary, for a letter arrangement in which the word spaces are as large or even larger than the line spaces is hard to read and seems disorderly.

Industrial Department   Industrial Department
Main Entrance   Main Entrance

Correct word and line spacing.   The word spacing is too large.
The arrangement falls apart.

SELECTION OF THE CORRECT LETTER STYLE

IN selecting a letter for a given task, beauty is not the only factor. The letter must also be appropriate to its purpose and surroundings. Most important, a distinction must be made between lettering that is to serve for a long period of time and lettering which is to serve only briefly. Frequently, we see lettering in architecture which, due to its flighty and cursive character, is suitable only for temporary and cheap signs. Many store front inscriptions, often excuted in metal or neon lights, belong to the category of imitation brush lettering which is alien to their purpose. These are not only generally hard to read, but also often lack the spontaneous, fresh form which only a master can give them after long practice. They are lame, warped, and miserable. That which one is unprepared to do but insists on doing becomes trashy. And this trash despoils our cities today at every turn. Such pap-like brush lettering on our store fronts is out of place and poorly done. Store front lettering is architecture, since it is a part of the building. It is destined for a long duration, often for decades, and should, therefore, always be correct, noble and beautiful. It is a waste of money to cast such pseudo brush lettering in expensive metal; it must be replaced in a few years as it becomes obsolete and visually offensive to everybody.

This kind of lettering is either the result of the client's "design" or conceived by incompetents who should choose another profession. The task is not that simple. Not everyone can do good lettering; as in painting, there are only a few masters.

To apply lettering to a building – and a store is part of a building – means applying an important element of the total appearance of the building and, for that matter, the appearance of the entire city. All lettering on buildings should therefore convincingly harmonize with the architecture. The ideal is lettering which becomes an ornament to the building and the store, whose loss would be felt.

First of all, the master of applied lettering will take a good look at the building and either obtain an elevation drawing or make one himself. It is not sufficient to look only at the store front. From across the street and beyond, one sees the entire building, not just the store. This is also true if the store, itself, is entirely modern in design while the building above is decorated in an earlier style. A master should therefore be well acquainted with architectural history. For only if he is able to tell the style and date of a building, can he find the appropriate lettering.

Even good antique letters seem strange on entirely modern buildings, and on buildings which are older than fifty years, letters like Gill Sans Serif (204, 205) are totally out of place. Faces of this kind are entirely appropriate only for buildings of pure modern style (as pioneered by Le Corbusier); however these letters are not the only ones suitable for such structures. The sober plainness and functional severity of modern architecture often demand a more refined, livelier, and richer letter form. But this means precisely the opposite of a tortured, flabby brush lettering imitation – a Didot (176, 177) or Bodoni (172–175) or the Trajan letter

(50 to 53). The beauty of these noble forms shines in its full glory on a sober, stark background, while a sans serif, particularly a heavy one, will easily look coarse and unappealing. The correct, that is sufficiently large, distance between letters is, of course, important here (see page 30–32).

For a building of the early nineteenth century a letter of that period is best. This calls primarily for Bodoni (172), Didot (176), Walbaum (180) and rarely their Italic. Buildings of the time around 1840 may be inscribed with Gras Vibert (182) or other letters of the period between 1820 and 1860. A sans serif of modern design such as Gill Sans Serif (204, 205) would not be suitable here. A condensed Gothic, a typical and rather attractive letter of the second half of the nineteenth century (194), is very suitable for most buildings of the period from 1840 to 1900.

The over-all proportions of the building inscription or store front lettering in relation to the surrounding features and prominent lines of the architecture is generally poorly thought out and ugly. The letters are usually far too large! They are, furthermore, generally placed far too close together and are difficult to read. Lettering of this kind also spoils our streets and daily offends our eye. The ugliness of most of our business streets is largely the result of oversized lettering, to say nothing of the incompetently designed letter forms. Thoughtless architects share the blame. But a refined inscription that is not vulgar and ostentatious can save a poorly designed store front and even give it charm. Almost all roman styles harmonize better with a building front than do the sans serifs. It is high time to call a halt to the spread of sans serifs in architecture and elsewhere.

The lettering must subordinate itself to the architecture and must not be allowed to overshadow it. This is where the conscientious letter designer or the architect must often overrule the client. The best argument to unreasonable wishes is that a perfectly arranged, subdued lettering is more 'modern' than a clumsy and oversized one, and it need only be legible at a distance of eight to twenty yards. Correctly spaced capitals, furthermore, are much more legible than word images that are too tight and thus unclear.

The exaggerated size of most letters makes it hard to read the message they are supposed to convey. Store and building signs are necessary, but they need not result in the evil they have become. Where community spirit and a sense of civic responsibility prevail, an appeal to reason is usually sufficient. Where these virtues are less developed, municipal bodies should be established to assure that public signs, billboards and lettering are in good taste and to prevent even minor excesses. Regulations regarding the size of signs are not sufficient. Such municipal bodies should employ graphic artists of high caliber or architects with an extensive knowledge of lettering. The appearance of cities, particularly cities that are being renewed, would then be improved noticeably in a few years.

THE most beautiful lettering is of little avail unless it is attractively arranged. The illustration below shows a slightly reduced copper engraving of the year 1640. The layout of the five lines is as perfect as the form of the individual letters and their even and beautiful spacing. We are dealing here with letters of two sizes which are clearly, but not grossly, different. The decision of the writing-master Francisco Pisano to use only two letter sizes for his text is worth imitating. Often too many letter sizes are used for the same job. It is one of the important secrets of good lettering layout to use as few letter sizes and styles as possible in one design. Those

who observe this rule can count on good results. The rule also has practical advantages; it is far simpler to work with only two or three sizes rather than five or six.

The example also shows a harmonious relationship between letter size and line spacing. The spacing between the first and second line is rightly just a little larger than the spacing between the other lines. The arrangement of the letters is perfect because it fills the given space unobtrusively and convincingly.

Two letter sizes are not always sufficient for the layout. But the rule should be no more than three. Three sizes permit as good a solution of all conceivable problems as the use of four or more. The necessity for a fourth size is rare. We comprehend the message and its significance not because of the size of the letters but because of their arrangement. Appropriate spacing can convey the logical meaning.

The two letter sizes of the Pisano copper engraving might be termed its two elements. If, instead of the smaller letter size, we were to use lower case letters of the size of the first line, we would deal with only one letter size but with what amounts to two elements. The harmony of the engraving is based on the similar form of all its letters. The harmony of the next example is based on the use of the same letter size in the capitals in the first line as in the lower case letters in the lines below. This example, too, is a model of a perfect, simple lettering solution. It does not have quite the formal effect of the historic example, but formality is not always in order. Informal uses demand somewhat more informal lettering designs.

We have learned that, rather than count letter sizes, we should speak of elements. This term seems necessary since roman letters can be used in two ways which have a rather different effect: as capitals alone and as capitals with lower case letters. The fact that we can achieve different effects with one size of roman letters, as we have seen in the last example, is another one of its great advantages.

If a layout begins with a small size, followed by a large one which, in turn is followed by the "same" size, we find that we shall have to use a third size to

---

FRANCISCUS PISANUS
scriptor genuensis sibi suisque
haeredibus vivens posuit
anno domini mdcxxxx

---

achieve the desired effect. On the door sign "Rentsch" shown on page 44, the bottom line seems to be as large as the top one. It is, however, smaller, although not much. We are dealing with three elements which appear as two elements. It would be ugly, incidentally, to letter space the top line to the full length of the white line. And if we were to enlarge the letter size to attain the full length of the white line, we would not achieve the desired effect. These are fine points.

It is generally wrong to letter space lines not containing exactly the same number of characters to the same width just in order to achieve a squared off effect. We must follow the rule that lines consisting of letters of the same size in the same arrangement must, under all circumstances, have the same letter spacing.

ARCHITECTURAL	ARCHITECTURAL
D E S I G N	DESIGN
Unsatisfactory.	Correct.
The letter spacing of letters of the same size in the same layout must be the same.	Identical letter spacing in both lines.

The following example shows a small group of letters in good and bad arrangements. In both instances the same size is used. In the left layout the characters and the lines are too close together and are hard to read. As we saw earlier, capital letters should not be used in such a clumsy manner. They must always be letter spaced. The smaller example at right is not only more legible, even though the letters are small, but is also more beautiful. The line spacing which is too tight at left is now equal to the letter size.

EXHIBITION
OPEN
10 A. M. – 5 P. M.

EXHIBITION
OPEN
10 A. M. — 5 P. M.

A letter jungle. Both the letters and the lines are too close. Hard to read.

Clear, legible and attractive due to generous letter spacing and line spacing.

It is a mistake to attempt to put the largest possible letter on a given space. Lettering does not increase in legibility with increased letter size, as most people seem to assume. The selection of the maximum size usually leads to letter spacing which is much too tight. Our streets are full of examples of this kind. Well spaced lettering is not only more attractive and more legible but also goes well with architecture. Poor lettering, which is too compressed and too large, is ugly and spoils our cities.

BAKERY

BAKERY

Ugly. The letters are too large and too close together in too small a space.

Smaller but well spaced and elegant letters delight the eye and are legible.

Beautiful Proportions of Signs

The over-all available space on which the lettering is placed is not always prescribed. It is then up to the designer to determine the size and proportion of the sign. These elements are far more important to the good appearance of the sign than is commonly assumed. A well proportioned background is necessary if a beautiful letter is to achieve its full effect. Signs which are perfectly square are generally ugly. A sign must be either long or tall. It is well to remember that exact geometric proportions, such as 1 : 2, 3 : 5 or the proportions of the Golden Section (about 21 : 34) are better and more beautiful than proportions which only approach these precise relationships. The illustration on the top of page 44 shows a sign in the exact proportion 3 : 5.

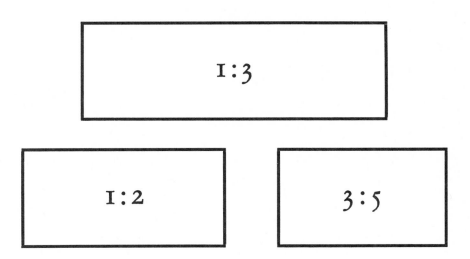

The reason that older buildings, including those of the late nineteenth century, seem more beautiful than some recent structures is due to the fact that their fenestration and their entire linear system are based on these tried and true proportions. Recently, the well-founded rules of proportion, which were followed in the Gothic and Renaissance periods, have been tossed out in the belief that intuition is sufficient. However, we are not born with a proper sense of proportion but must slowly develop it like good taste. Proportions alone do not create art, but they are a good test for all graphic work including lettering.

Trademark and door sign for a printing firm, designed by the author.
Gold letters on black background.
Actual size approximately 20″ × 13″.

Trademark for the Basle lithographer and offset printer Morf, designed by the author.
Hand lithography is symbolized by the use of the elegant Anglaise script.
Offset printing is symbolized by the three cylinders which are characteristic of that process.

About the Ampersand

Nowadays the symbol &, which appears on most of the plates of this book, is used in place of the word "and" in the name of firms. It is an old "connected letter" or ligature. It contains the often barely recognizable two letters e and t from the Latin word meaning 'and'. Old forms of this symbol are found on pages 57, 80, 81, 127, 129, 132 and 135. The handsome forms of the great calligrapher Lucas Materot occasionally reveal the two letters quite clearly. Except in firm names which consist of the names of persons, this symbol should not replace the spelled out "and." In the name "Paper and Cardboard Company" the word "and" should not appear in the form of the ampersand, even if the designation is part of the firm name and

not just an explanation. The ampersand should be used only between personal names such as Miller & Furrer. Lately one unfortunately also sees the plus symbol, +, instead of &. This is wrong. School children may say "and" instead of "plus" when they enunciate the plus symbol, but "Miller plus Furrer" is incorrect. Mr. Furrer is not added to Mr. Miller but both rank equally and form the association "Miller & Furrer."

The plus sign is used by sign painters and graphic artists who probably do not know how to handle the ampersand. They use an improper simplification. Trademarks, too, should not use the plus sign instead of the ampersand. People who do not wish to paint or draw an ampersand should not attempt lettering.

THE PLATES

MEMORIAE
RVFINA TONE GRECO
MYLA SIC CHORVLE
QVI VIXII ANNOS
XVI DIONYSIVS
ASCLEPIADES NATI
ONE ALEXANDRI
NVS PARENS IT
ATHENEVS BENEM
RENTI   DES

VS·POPVLVSQ

ARI·DIVI·N

O·AVG·GER

·TRIB·POT·XV

RANDVM·QVA

·VSTAN·

51

ABC
DEF
GHIJ
KLM

NOP
QRS
TUW
XYZ

QVISSINECPOTVERE
VOMISETINFLEXIPRIMV
TARDAQELEVSINEMATR
TRIBVLAEQTRAHAEQETI
VIRGEAPRAETEREADEL

PICIENSSVMMAFLAVVMCA
OCVLOGEMITVNONERVSTRA
NESORORIPSETIBITVAMAX
ISARISTAEVSPENEIGENITOR
pp vano pena
ACRIMANSETTECRVDELEM

SVNTETSPIRITIBVSSAEPENOCENTIBVS
POENARVMCELEBRESSVBSTYGITRI
ILLANOCTESACERQVAREDIITDEVS
STAGNISADSVPEROSEXACKERVNT
NONSICVTTENEBRASDEFACEFVLGIDA
SVRGENSOCEANOLVCIFERINBVIT

54

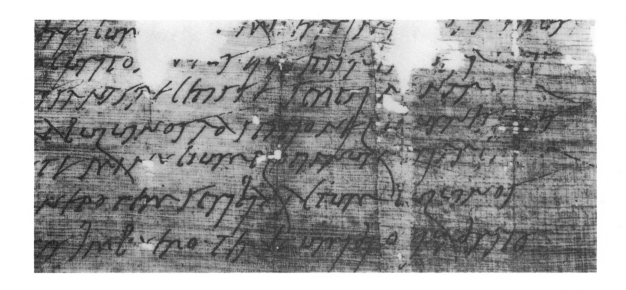

MINISUENIENTE
INNUBIBUSCAE
LICUMUIRTUTE
MULTAETMAIES
TATEETMITITAN
GELOSSUOSCUM
TUBAETUOCEMAG
NAETCONGREGA

BULAMCUMIAM
RAMUSILLIUSTUE
RITTENEREITFOLIA
NATAFUERINTCOG
NOSCITISPROPE
ESSEAESTATEM
SICETUOSCUMUI
DERITISHAECOM

TRANSIERUNTIORDANE
ETABIERUNTTOTAMPRAE
TENTURAM ETUENERUN
INCASTRAMADIAM ET
IOABREUERSUSESTDE
POSTABENNER ETCON
GRAECARUNTTOTUM
POPULUM ETUISISUN

INTO
ETD
CEB
ETI
TISU
ehe
mic
mo

ᵥOMNIA ERGO QUAECU
TIS UT FACIANT UOBIS
ET UOS FACITE EIS hA
ᴸᵛ   LEX ET PROPHET
ᵥINTRATE PERANGUSTA̅

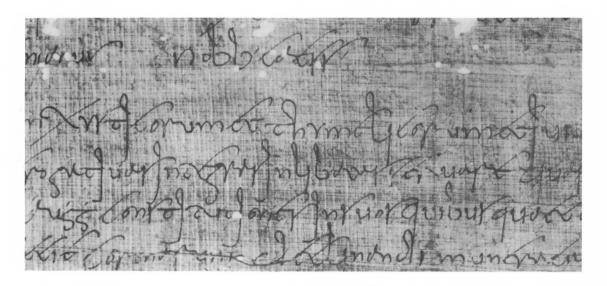

ex hebraeo interpretantur proben t nobis hoc se
quod interpretantur et septuaginta interpretan
quae tanto et tam diuinitur facto miraculo comme
tur necclesii fuctus tace firmetur ;
        De luca quod fecit ioseph patri suo sep teme
ˣᶜᴵᴵ   ex eodem libro quaestionum de zenesi
Et fecit luctum patri suo septem dies. nescio utrum
alicui conorum in scribtaris celebratum esse luca
quod apud latinos nouendial appellant; unde mi
ab hac consuetudine prohibendi siqui xp̄iano nō
tur is sui numerum seruant quia magis festa ingent

spiam alligatam & pullum cum ea

soluite & adducite mihi. Et si

quis uobis aliquid dixerit dicite

quoniam his opus habet & confestim

omnia eos

Autem factum est totum

pleretur quod dictum est

pphetam prophetam dicentem dia

te phuaesion ecce rex tuus uenit

tibi mansuetus & sedens super

in quit agnaf accipief de manum mea . ut fint in teftimo
nium mihi qrm ego fodi puteum iftum . Idcirco
uocatuf e locuf ille berfabee . quia ibi uterque
iurauit . & inierunt foeduf pro puteo iuramenta
Surrexit autem abimelech & ficol princeps militie
eiuf . reuerfi quefunt in terram paleftinorum .
Abraham uero plantauit nemuf in berfabee . & in
uocauit ibi nomen dni di aeterni . & fuit terrae
colonuf philiftinorum diebuf multif .
Quae poftquam gefta funt . temptauit df abraham .
& dixit ad eu . Abraham . ille refpondit . Adfu .
Ait illi . Tolle filium tuum unigenitu quem dili
gif ifaac . & uade in terra uifionif atq: offer eum
ibi holocauftum fuper unum montium quem
monftrauero tibi . Igitur abraham de nocte con
furgenf ftrauit afinum fuum ducenf fecu duof
iuuenef . & ifaac filium fuu . Cumq: concidiffet
ligna in holocauftum . abiit ad locum quem prae
ceperat ei df . Die autem tertio leuatif oculif .
uidit locum procul . Dixitque ad pueros fuof
Exfpectate hic cum afino . ego & puer illuc ufque
properantef . poftquam adorauerimuf reuerte
mur ad uof . Tulit quoque ligna holocaufti . &
inpofuit fuper ifaac filium fuum . Ipfe uero
portabat in manib: fuif ignem & gladium . Cu
que duo pergerent fimul . dixit ifaac patri fuo
Pater mi . at ille refpondit . Quid uif fili . ~ Ecce

Cognouit ergo turba multa ex iudaeis quia illic est · et ueneri
non propter ihm tantum · sed ut lazarum uiderent quem sus
citauit a mortuis · Cogitauerunt autem principes sacer
dotum · ut et lazarum interficerent · quia multa propter illu
abibant ex iudaeis et credebant in ihm ·

IN CRASTINUM AUTE TURBA MULTA
quae uenerat ad diem festum cum audissent quia uenit ihc
hierosolimam · acceperunt ramos palmarum · et processer
obuiam ei et clamabant · O sanna benedictus qui uenit in
nomine dni rex istrahel ·

Et inuenit ihc asellum · et sedit super eum · sicut scriptum est ·
Noli timere filia sion · ecce rex tuus uenit sedens suppullu asine
haec non cognouerunt discipuli eius primu · sed quando glori
ficatus est ihc · tunc recordati sunt quia haec erant scripta
de eo · et haec fecerunt ei · Testimonium ergo per hibebat
turba quae erat cum eo quando lazarum uocauit de monu
mento · et suscitauit eum a mortuis · Propterea et obuia
uenit ei turba · quia audierunt eum fecisse hoc signum ·

Pharisaei ergo dixerunt ad semetipsos · uidetis quia nihil
proficimus · ecce mundus totus post eum abit · Erant aute
gentiles quidam ex his qui ascenderant · ut adorarent in
die festo · hi ergo accesserunt ad philippum qui erat ab eth
saida galileae · et rogabant eum dicentes · Dne uolumus ihm
uidere · Uenit philippus et dicit andree · andreas rursu

FESTIS · APRBISAUTÉ
MINIMEDICITUR · NISI
SOLOINPASCHA · QUAN
DOUEROLAETANIAAGI
TURNEQUEGLORIAIN
EXCELSISDONEQUEALL
CANTUR POSTMODŪ
DICITURORATIO · DEIN
DESEQUITURAPOSTO
LUS ITEMGRADALIS
SIUEALLELUIA POST
MODUM LEGITUR EU
ANGELIUMDEINDEOF
FERTORIŪETDICITUR
ORATIOSUPEROBLATA
QUACŌPLETADICIT SACER
DOSEXCELSAUOCE ·

60

CAPITULA IUNIORIS KAROLI REGIS·
IN PISTIS FACTA

KAROLVS
GRATIA
DI REX

Notu esse uolumus omnib; di & nris fidelibus qm haec quae secuntur captaula nunc in isto placito nro· Anno ab incarnatione edni nri ihuxpi Dcccc Lxiiii· Anno uidelicet regni nri ipso propitio xxv Inditione xij· vii kl iul in hoc loco quidi citur pistus una cu fideliu nroru consensu atq, consilio constituimus & cunctis sineulla refragatione perregnu nrm obseruanda mandamus·

Primo considerauimus dehonore ecclesiaru & sacerdotu ac seruoru di & Inmuni tate reru ecclesiasticaru ut nullus sibi deipsis rebus contra auctoritate presumat· & comites epis eu ministris ecclae Ineoru minis teriis adiutores inomnab. fiant· sicut incaptulari predecessoru ac pro genitoru nroru continetur Insecundo libro cap xxiii Etquiaiq, co mitu uel ministroru reipublicae haec quae mandamus obseruare negle xerit· siprima & secunda uice dehis admonitus nonsecorrexerit· uo lumus utneglegentia comitis adnram notitiam perepos etpermissos nros deferatur· & alioru neglegentia percomites adnram notitiam

SCDM. IOHANNEM.

N PRINCIPO

ERAT VERBV

ET VERBVM ERAT

APVD DEVM. ET DEVS ERAT

uerbum. hoc erat inprincipi
.o apud dm. Omnia p ipfum
facta funt. & fine ipfo factum
eft nihil. Quod factum eft.
inipfo uita erat. Et uita
erat lux hominum. & lux in
tenebrif lucet. & tenebre eam
non comprehenderunt. Fuit
homo miffuf adeo. cui nomen
erat Iohs. Hic uenit intefti
moniū ut teftimonium perhi

62

ille tie pstratz uemã postulat culpã ofi
tetur. pniam iplozat. te sutis cautelã
spontet. tuc est appbensa manu et ter
tera. eccam eu introdu cat.⁊ coione̅ xpi
anã ei redvat. vii. ps. pni ales tecantan
do cu parb₂. Byuel⁊ at ni: ⁊c. ut̅s Ore̅
aieftatem tuam qs dñe sce pat ozo.
Oompr etie t̅s. qui nõ moztem pror
sz uemam semp iquins. respice flente̅
famulu̅ tuu̅. attente pstratu̅. euusqp
planctu̅ i gaudiu̅ tue miseratois cõ
uerte. scm te delictoz sactu̅.⁊ indue eu̅
leticia salutari. ut pp longam pegrin
atõnis fame̅ te scis altarib₂ satietur.
ingissusqp cubiculu̅ regis i ipsis aula
bindicat nome̅ glie tue semp. p.x.v.n.
re Am̅. al'. ozoz O eus miseri cozs teus
clemes. ize. v. feř. v. tene dñi. uerb plura
lis num eri i singlare mutatis. ❡ Oztvav
recocuanv apostatã. scismaticu̅.
postate recocili ❡ ul hereticaz.
atõ sit h movo. primo ei ante

Grymiger abtilger aller leut ſchedlicher echʒ vñ
veruolger aller werlt · Fraiſſamer moꝛder aller
mēſchē · Ir tod euch ſei verflucht got eur ſtraffer haſʒ
euch unſeldē merūg woͤ pei euch ungeluck hauſʒ ge
waltiglich zu euch zu mal geſchēt ſeit ymer · Angſt
not vñ iamer verlaſſē euch nicht wo ir wāderr · laid
betrupnuſʒ vñ auch kumer beleitē euch allenthalbē
leidige anfechtūg · ſchētliche zuuſicht und ſchēliche
anferūg die betwingē euch grobliche̅ an aller ſtat ·
Himel · erdē · ſuñ · mon · geſtirn · mer · wagk · perg · ge
fild · tal · awe · der helle abgrūt · auch alles das leben
und weſen hat ſey euch unholt ungūſtig vñ fluchē
ewiglichē · In poſʒheit verſincket in iemerlichē elend
verſchwynder und in der unwiderpringlichē ſchwerſtē
echt gottes aller leut und iglicher geſchepfūg aller
zukūfftiger zeit beleibt unūſchamter poſʒwicht · eur
poſe gedechtnuſʒ · Ieb und trauer hin an end · grau
und vorcht ſcheidē voͤ euch nicht wo ir wandert · vñ
wonet von mir und aller meniglich ſei ſteriglichen
geſchriē vber euch ernſtlichē zeter geſchrei mit gewū
den henden · ⁌ Des tods wider red das ander capitel ·
Hort hort hort new wunder grauſʒā und unge
hort teiding vechten uns an · von wem die ku
mē das iſt uns zu mal ſer fremd · Doch treuēs · fluch
ens · zetter geſchreis · hendwindēs · und allerlei antri
gens ſein wir elender untz her wol geneſen · Dēnach
ſun wer du piſt mell dich vñ lautmer was dir leidēs
von uns widerfarn ſei · Darumb du uns ſo unzemli

64

Ioseph quid agis, Ré profecto oparis
q̃ me profundissima admiratōe suspē
dit, herodem timens ne puerum perdat,
in egiptuz cum puero ⁊ matre eius fugis
O res stupenda nonne puer iste est paruu
lus ille qui paucos ante dies natus est no
bis, cuius imperiuz ut propheta sanctus
ait super humersi eius, deus fortis pater
futuri seculi, princeps pacis, Nimis profecto arbitratus es herodis potētiā, ut me-
tueres ne paruulū pderet, cui est potestas
immēsa, maiestas infinita, et insupabilis

C Das Erst blat   C Das erst büch
ein über grosse teüre·sterbent·vnd tod sucht·darüber hetten
sÿ rat des gotes appolinis·do funden sÿ das sÿ die sel esopi
sölten gütigen vnd versönen·Dö wurden sÿ reüwig daz sÿ
esopum vnschuldigklich heten getödtet·vnd baweten jm
einen neüen tempel·vnd zů seiner ewigen gedächtnuß liefs/
sen sÿ jm ein saule darein setzen·über das·do die fürsten võ
kriechenlandt den tode Esopi erhözten zugtent sÿ in hözes
kraft über die delphen·vnd erfüren fleÿssigklichen wöliche
schuld hettent an dem tod esopi dÿe liessent sÿ all als billich
was mit sölichem tod auch vergeen·
    C Hie hat ein ende das lesen esopi·
    C Die vozrede Romuli philosophi in das büch Esopi·

Romulus seinem sun von der stat athemis heÿl·Eso
pus ist gewesen ein simreÿcher man auß kriechen
der durch sein fabeln die menschē gelert hat·wie sÿ
sich in allem thůn vnd lassen halten söllen·Aber darum das
er das leben der menschen vnd auch jre sitten erzeÿgen mö
chte hat er in seinen fabeln redent·vogel·bäum·wÿlde vnd
zäme thÿer·hÿrß·wolff·fuchs·lewen·schaff·geÿß·vnd an
dere gezogen nach gebürlicheÿt einer ÿeden fabel·darauß
man leicht vnd verstentlich erkennen mag·warūb dÿe ge/
                                            ·e·iiij·

66

Register Des
buchs der Cro=
niken vnd geschichten
mit figurn vnd pildnis
sen von anbegyn der welt
bis auf dise vnsere Zeit

vanden poozten eñ dedenſe wyde opē
doe quamē ſy al inne. ende doe ſloegē
ſij die turcken doot in allē plecken. Eñ
caſſiaen die coninc van Antiochien ōt=
vloot. maer hy wert ghegrepen van=
den ſaraſinen die hi gheuangen hielt
die hem ſijn hoot afſloeghen eñ brach
ten dat den kerſtenen. Aldus wert die
ſtad gewonnen int iaer M. eñ xcviij.
op eenen donredach voir oogſt na dat
ſy. ix. maenden belegē hadde geweeſt.
daer ſy niet vele vitalien en vondē. eñ
cume hddden ſy. ij. C. peerden mager
eñ ongeuallich.

℄ Des ſaterdaechs daer na quā voer
die ſtad Cozbohan die coninc vā cozo=
ſaim. om die kerſten te beuechtene eñ
hy belach die ſtad mettē voerſ coninc
Saleman. want hy wyſte wel datter
niet meer volcks en quā wt kerſtērijc
ke. eñ dat die vitalie dunne was. ende
hy benam dat vander ſee hem gheen
nootdozft gecomē en conſte. Doe ledē
die kerſtene ſo groten hongher eñ ſulc
ken gebrecht inde ſtad. datter vele ſtoz
uen. eñ ſy aten peerden. mule. eſelen.
kemelen. eñ doode honden die ſy ſoden
Aldus en hadden ſy gheen hope dā op
gode alleen. Als ſy in deſen noode wa=
ſo en waſſer nyet vele ſy en haddē wel
willen vlieden. Doe was daer eē goet
gheeſtelijck clerck wt Lombaerdiē die
den gheeſt gods hadde. die bat dē hee=
ren dat ſy hē hoozen wouden ſpreken
Daer vtelde hy van eenē goeden prieſ
ter wt Italien dien hy goet van leuen
kinde die welcke int beghin van deſer
vaert op eē tijt als hi ouer wech ghieck
ter plaetſen weert daer hi miſſe ſingē
ſoude. ontmoette eenen pelgreē die hē

aen ſprack vander cruyſuaert die doe
begonſte. ſeggende datſe van god ghe
ozdyneert was. die pyeſter ſeyde. hoe
weetti dat. die pelgrem antwoorde. Ic
ben Ambzoſius byſſcop van Milanē
Ende dit licteeken ſeldy den kerſtenen
dzaghen. Ouer. iiij. Iaren van deſen
dage ſal god den kerſtenen gheuē Ihe
ruſalem. Ende met dien woozden ver
ſchiet ſinte Ambzoſius vā daer. Doen
ſeyde voozt die voozſeyde goede clerck
totten kerſtenē. Het is gheleden twee
iaren dat dit gheſchiedde. eñ this te ho
pen dattet int eyde niet ſaillyerē en ſal
Bi deſen woozdē wert dat volc alſoe v
trooſt eñ geſterct datſe nymmermeer
vlyen en woudē

℄ Item eenē anderē goeden prieſtere
opēbaerde haer ōs lieue vzouwe met
haren kinde Iheſu eñ met ſinte peter
Ende hem werdt gheſeyt dat hi tot dē
kerſtenē ſegghen ſoude datſe hem be=
keeren ſouden tot gode: aflegghende
haer ſonden. ende datſe god dan vhoo
ren ſoude.

℄ Itē oec ſo openbaerde ſinte Andries
eenē goeden clerc wt Prouenciē eñ hy
wijſde hem een ſtede in ſinte Peeters
kercke tot Anthiochyē: daer den ſpeer
ons liefs heeren iheſu criſti begrauen
lach. Ende men vantten met grooter
blijſſchappē. ende met groter deuociē
werdt hi gheeert

℄ Doe wardē die kerſtene princen be=
raden wt te trecken tſeghē den coninc
Cozboham. dieſe dzye wekē beleghen
hade met groter menichten van volc
ke ſo ſtranghelijc datter niemant dan
god almachtich hem ghehulpē en kō
de. Die kerſtenē biechteden hem ende
N

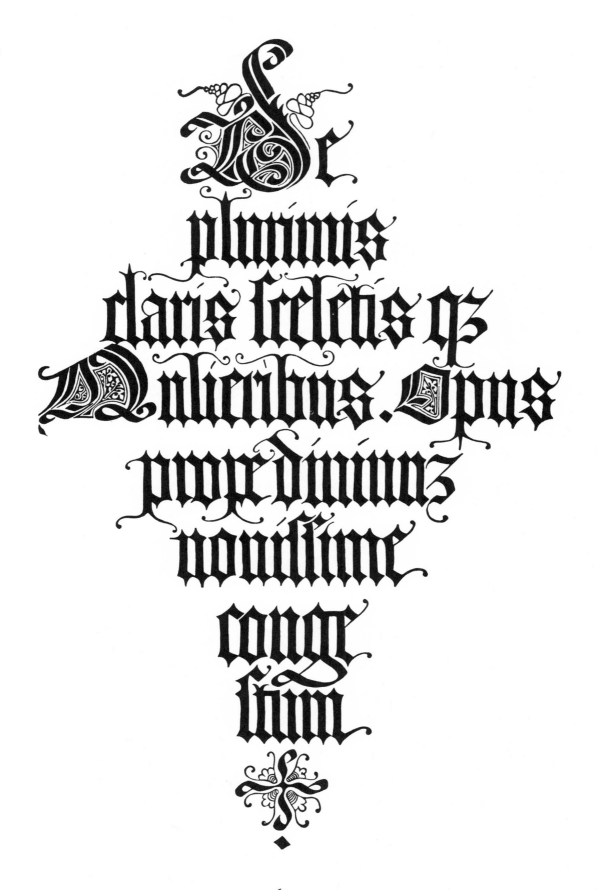

De
plurimis
claris sclctis g
Mulieribus. Opus
prope diuinuz
nouissime
coge
stum

Confiteant̃ dño mlscdie eius :
lia eius filijs hominũ, Ut facri
ficiũ laudis:⁊ annũcient opera e
tatione, Qui descendũt mare in
faciẽtes opratione in aquis mul
viderũt opa dñi: et mirabilia eiu
do, Dixit et stetit spirit⁹ prelle
ti sũt fluctus eius Afcendũt ulǫ
et descendunt usǫ ad abissos : a
in malis tabelscebat, Turbati l
funt sicut ebrius: et omnis sapiĩ
uozata est, Et clamauerũt ad i
tribularent̃ : et de necessitatibꝫ e
eos, Et statuit procellam eius in
luerũt fluctus eius, Et letati su

A B C D E F G H J L

N A O P R S T V X

a b c d d d d a w e f f a f g h i

i j l m n o p q r w s s f f f ß t

w u v x p z ꝯ . : ⸗

Exoretur deus pro anima quondam dñi
Johannis nygendorp: perpetui dux vixit
in ecclesia Hamburgeñ Vicarij. Pro cuius salute hec beate Marie compassionis
instituta est memoria. Impressag in im-
periali ciuitate Lubeck. Arte ⁊ Ingenio
Stephani arndes: Anno dñi millesimo-
quadringentesimo Nonagesimoquinto
Vigesimaoctaua die mensis Martij

caſtra regis. Janus vero filius vroſa: palatinus comes longe
deſcenderāt de rege. Qui cum audiſſent ſilēter vnanimiter ſuos
armauerūt z impetū ſup bohemos qui caſtra deuaſtabāt ſecerūt.
Contriuitqz dñs eos in oze gladij bungaroz z dira mozte ſaucia
uit. Miſitqz ianus poſt regē nūcium z manifeſtauit illi victozaz
quā dñs ſibi dederat. Rex itaqz reuerſus ganiſus eſt gaudio ma
gno: ſz valde doluit: qz ſoltb in eodem plio moztuus nó ſuit qui
tanta mala mendacijs ſimilabat: Rex aūt ſtephanus legittimaz
volebat ducere vxozem ſz cōcubinis meretricibus iunctus erat.
Quare barones z optimates dolētes de regni deſolatiōe z regꝰ
ſterilitate duxerūt ei vxozez dñam nobiliſſimam filiā regis rober
ti viſcardi de apulia: venit itaqz dux theutonicoz nomie Bezen
ad regem z conqueſtus ei eſt vt frater ſuus eū de ducatu eieciſſet.
roganſqz regis clementiā vt in ppzia pſona ſua ipſū adiuuaret.
Rex aūt ſtephanus nolēs iiuriā patris ſui regis Colomani vin
dicare pmiſit ducem adiuuatuz. z collecto exercitu iuit in ruſciaz
Cunqz pueniſſet primus obſedit caſtz. Contigit aūt ſummo di
luculo qp poictus dux Bezen ambulabat circa caſtruz puidēdo
loca expugnandi munitiones. Obſeſſi vero exiuerant de caſtro
cauſa viſitandi bungaros. Cunqz dux vidiſſet illos impetuz ſe
cit ſup illos qui viriliter pugnantes ducem vſqz ad moztem vul
nerauerunt. Cunqz rex audiſſet de mozte ducis indignatus ē val
de z precepit omnibus bungaris vt caſtrum obpugnarēt z eodē
die elegerent munitiōes poſſidere vel mozi. Principes aūt bun
garie babuerunt conſiliū z dixerunt. Quid z quare mozimur: ſi
ducatuim vendicabimus quem rex ex nobis cōſtituet ducē. Sta
bilitum igiꝰ ſic inter nos qp nullus caſtrum obpugnet z dicamus
regi. Quia bec omnia abſqz conſilio ſuoz principum facit. Cuz
vero principes veniſſent ad conſilium regis omēs in duas par
tes ſe tranſtulerunt. Sed Cozma de genere paznā erexit ſe di
cens regi. Domine quid eſt quod facis: ſi cum multitudine moz
te militum tuozum caſtruz capis quem ducem conſtitues. Si in
ter principes tuos eligis nullus remanet. Nunquid vos vultꝰ
regno relicto babere ducatū: nos barones caſtz nó obpugnabi

72

Cum orationibus pulcherrimis dicendis circa agonizantem.

aut argumentoy aut sententiay : aut deniq descriptio
nis aut ordinis . fateamur aut hoc quod hec ars profiteat
alienum esse : aut cum alia aliqua arte esse comune . sed si
in hac una est ea ratio atq doctrina : non si qui aliay artiu
bene loquuti sunt : eo minus id est huius unius proprium
Sed ut orator de his rebus que ceteray artium sunt : si modo
eas cognouit . ut heri crassus dicebat : optime potest dicere .
sic ceteray artium hoies ornatius illa sua dicunt : siqd ab
hac arte didicerunt . Neq eim si de rebus rusticis agricola
qspiam : aut etiam id quod multi medici de morbis : aut de
pingendo pictor aliqs diserte dixerit aut scripserit : idcirco
illius artis putanda est eloquentia . in qua qa uis magna
est in hoium ingeniis : eo multi etiam sine doctrina aliqd
oium geney atq artium consequunt . sed quod cuiusq sit
proprium ! & si ex eo iudicari potest cum uideris quid queq
doceant : tamen hoc certius esse nihil potest : q quod oes
artes alie sine eloquentia suum munus prestare possunt :
orator sine ea nomen suum optinere non potest . Vt cete
ri si diserti sint aliqd ab hoc habeant : hic nisi domesticis
se instruxerit copiis aliunde dicendi copiam petere non
possit . Tum catulus : & si inqt antoni minime impediedus
est interpellatione iste cursus orationis tue : patiere tamen
mihiq ignosces . non eim possum quin exclamem ut ait ille
in trinumo : ita uim oratoris mihi tum exprimere subtili
ter uisus es : tum laudare copiosissime . Quod qdem eloque
tem uel optime facere oportet ut eloqntiam laudet . Debet

AGNO ET EXCELLENTI INGENIO VIRI cum se doctrinę penitus dedissent quicquid laboris poterat impendi contemptis omnibus ce priuatis ce publicis actionibus ad inquirende ueritatis studium contulerunt existimantes multo esse preclarius humanarum diuinaszq, rerum inuestigare ac scire rationem q̃ struendis opibus aut cumulandis honoribus inherere. Quibus rebus quoniam fragiles terreneq, sunt ce ad solius corporis pertinent cultũ nemo melior nemo iustior effici potest. Erant quidem illi ueritatis cognitione dignissimi quam scire tãtopere cupierunt atq, ita ut eam rebus omnibus anteponerent. Nam ce abiecisse quosdam res familiares suas ce renuntiasse uniuersis uoluptatibus constat. ut solam nudamq, uirtutem nudi expeditiq, sequerentur. Tantum apud eos uirtutis nomen ce auctoritas ualuit ut in ipã esse summi boni premium predicarent. Sed neq, adepti sunt id quod uolebãt ce operam simul atq, industriam perdiderunt. quia ueritas idest archanum sũmi dei qui fecit omnia ingenio ac propriis sensibus non potest comprehendi alioquin nichil inter deum ce hominem distaret. si consilia ce dispositiones illius maiestatis ecternę cogitatio assequeretur humana. Quod quia fieri non potuit. ut homini perse ipsum ratio diuina notesceret. non est passus hominem deus lumen sapientię requirentem diutius errare ac sine ullo laboris effectu uagari per tenebras inextricabiles. Aperuit oculos eius aliquando ce notionẽ ueritatis munus suum fecit. ut ce humanam sapientiam nullam esse monstraret ce erranti ac uago uiam consequendę immortalitatis ostenderet. oo. Verum quoniam pauci utuntur hoc cęlesti beneficio ac munere quod obuoluta in obscuro ueritas latet. ea quę uel contemptui doctis est quia idoneis assertoribus eget. Vel odio indoctis ob insitam sibi austeritatem quam natura hominum procliuis inuitia pati non potest. N̄ quia uirtutibus

qui omnibus ui aquarum submerſis cum filiis ſuis ſimul ac nuribus
mirabili quodā modo quaſi ſemen huāni generis conſeruatus eſt:quē
utinā quaſi uiuam quandam imaginem imitari nobis contingat:& hi
quidem ante diluuium fuerunt:poſt diluuium autem alii quorū unus
altiſſimi dei ſacerdos iuſtitiæ ac pietatis miraculo rex iuſtus lingua he
bræorū appellatus eſt:apud quos nec circuncſionis nec moſaicæ legis
ulla mentio erat . Quare nec iudæos(poſteris eni hoc nomen fuit)neq;
gentiles:quoniam non ut gentes pluralitatem deorum inducebant ſed
hebræos proprie noīamus aut ab Hebere ut dictū eſt:aut qa id nomen
tranſitiuos ſignificat.Soli qppe a creaturis naturali rōne & lege īnata
nō ſcripta ad cognitionē ueri dei trāſiere:& uoluptate corporis cōtēpta
ad rectam uitam pueniſſe ſcribunt:cum quibus omibus præclarus ille
totius generis origo Habraam numerādus eſt:cui ſcriptura mirabilem
iuſtitiā quā non a moſaica lege(ſeptima eīm poſt Habraā generatione
Moyſes naſcitur)ſed naturali fuit ratione conſecutus ſūma cum laude
atteſtatur.Credidit enim Habraam deo & reputatū eſt ei in iuſtitiam.
Quare multarum quoq; gentium patrem diuina oracula futurū:ac in
ipſo benedicēdas oēs gentes hoc uidelic& ipſum quod iam nos uideūs
aperte prædictum eſt:cuius ille iuſtitiæ perfectioēm non moſaica lege
ſed fide cōſecutus eſt:qui poſt multas dei uiſiones legittimum genuit
filium:quem primum omnium diuino pſuaſus oraculo circūcidit:&
cæteris qui ab eo naſcerétur tradidit:uel ad manifeſtum multitudinis
eorum futuræ ſignum:uel ut hoc quaſi paternæ uirtutis iſigne filii re
tinétes maiores ſuos imitari conaret:aut qbuſcūq; aliis de cauſis.Non
enim id ſcrutādum nobis modo eſt.Poſt Habraam filius eius Iſaac in
pietate ſucceſſit:fœlice hac hæreditate a parétibus accæpta:q uni uxori
coniunctus quum geminos genuiſſet caſtitatis amore ab uxore poſtea
dicitur abſtinuiſſe.Ab iſto natus ē Iacob qui ppter cumulatū uirtutis
prouétum Iſrael etiam appellatus eſt duobus noībus ppter duplicem
uirtutis uſū.Iacob eīm athletā & exercétem ſe latine dicere poſſumus:
quam appellatiōe primū habuit:quū practicis operatioībus multos
pro pietate labores ferebat.Quum autē iam uictor luctando euaſit:&
ſpeculationis fruebat bonis:tūc Iſraelem ipſe deus appellauit æterna
premia beatitudinéq; ultimam quæ in uiſione dei conſiſtit ei largiens:
hominem enim qui deum uideat Iſrael nomen ſignificat. Ab hoc.xii.
iudæorum tribus pfectæ ſūt.Innumerabilia de uita iſtorum uirorum
fortitudine prudentia pietateq; dici poſſunt:quorum alia ſecundum
ſcripturæ uerba hiſtorice conſiderantur:alia tropologice ac allegorice
interpretat:de qbus multi cōſcripſerūt:& nos in libro quē inſcripſiūs

FELICE
FELICIANO
ABCDE
FGHIJKLM
NOPQ
RSTUVW
XYZ

hostes. seu qui militant contra
inuidiam diabolorum. aut
qui uotum uouerint domi-
no cantare cotidie integrum
psalterium. et non possunt.
aut qui ieiunant et ieiunio
nimium debilitantur etq̃
festa solennia non custodiut
et qui animam suam saluā
uolunt facere secundum mi
sericordiam dei. Et uitam
eterna uolunt habere. assidue

cantent hoc psalterium. et
possidebunt regnum eternū.
Vscipe digneris do[mine] Oro
mine deus omnipotens
istos psalmos consecratos q̃s
ego indignus decantare cu
pio in honore nominis tui
domine. beatę marię uirgi
nis et omnium sanctorum
tuorum. pro me miserimo
Euanzelista famulo tuo: et p
genitore meo et genitrice mā.

meorum. Illumina faciem
tuam super seruum tuum. &
saluum me fac in misericor
dia tua non confundar quo
niam inuocaui te. Benedi
cam dominum in omni tem
pore semper laus eius i ore
meo. In domino laudabi
tur anima mea audiant mā
sueti et letentur. Magnifi
cate dominum mecum et
exaltemus nomen eius in

id ipsum. Iudica domine
nocentes me expugna expu
gnantes me. Apprehende
arma et scutum et exurge in
adiutorium mihi. Ne sileas
domine ne discedas a me.
exurge; et intende iudicio
meo domine deus meus Pre
tende misericordiam tuam.
hijs qui recto sunt corde. Nō
ueniát mihi pes superbię et
manus peccatoris non moue

Verum qui parum a recto exorbitat : non carpit̄
siue' ad defectum : siue' ad exsuperationem se'flec-
tat : qui uero multum : uituperatur. non enim latet egressus . Facile' autem non est excipere' ratione'
quousq̃ et ad quantum a recto quispiam egressus
carpendus est . Neq̃ enim aliud quicquam sensi-
bilium determinari facile' potest . Talia uero in
singulis sunt et iudicium est in sensu. Verum il-
lud est manifestum medium habitum in uniuersis
laudabilem esse' . Oportet autem nunc ad exsuperationem : nunc ad defectum declinare' . hoc enim
modo facillime' medium ipsum et rectum attinge-
mus et assequemur : ~

ETHICORVM
LIBRI TERTII
CAPVT · I ·

VM VIRTVS
circa affectus actusq̃ uer-
setur : et in ijs quidem quæ'
sua sponte' quis agit laudes
et uituperationes : in ijs au-
d 2

Deo optimo & Immortali auspice :-

abcdefgghiklmnopqrstuxx
xyyzττσ

Ofia il stato humani. Chi questa sera finise
il corso suo. (Si diman nase. Sol
virtu doma Morte horrida
e, altera.

Hæc tirus Romæ in Parhione
scribeba.

· ANN · M D XXII ·
Deo, & Virtuti omnia debent,

Reginam illam procacium nitidore Auaritia
cui cuncta crimina detestabili deuotione
famulantur,
eug; quidem Auari=
tia
fuge,

Studium pecuniæ habet, quam nemo Sa=
piens concupiuit: Ea quasi malis ve=
nenis imbuta, corpus animumg;
virilem effæmi=
nat

neg; copia neg; inopia minuitur

Auarus i nullo bonus i seaut pessimus :-

80

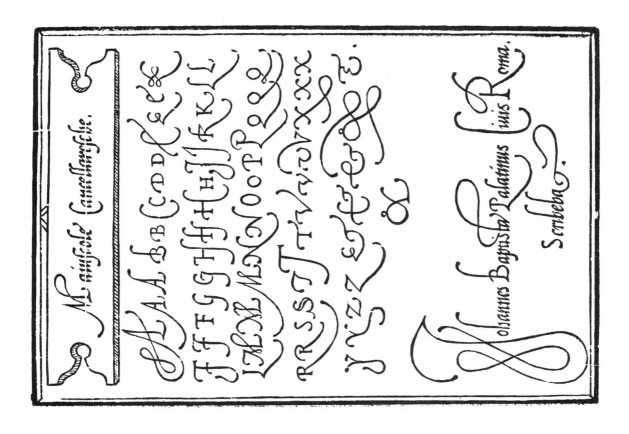

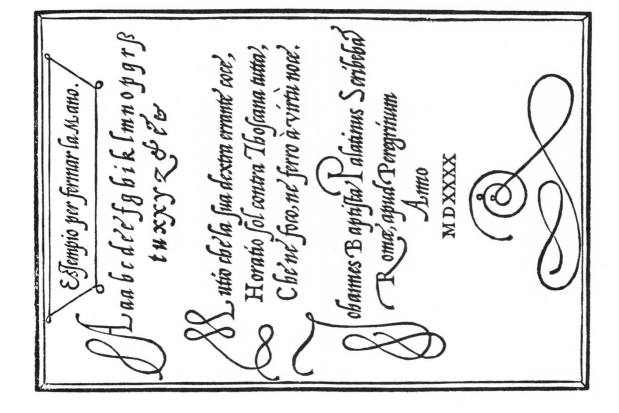

81

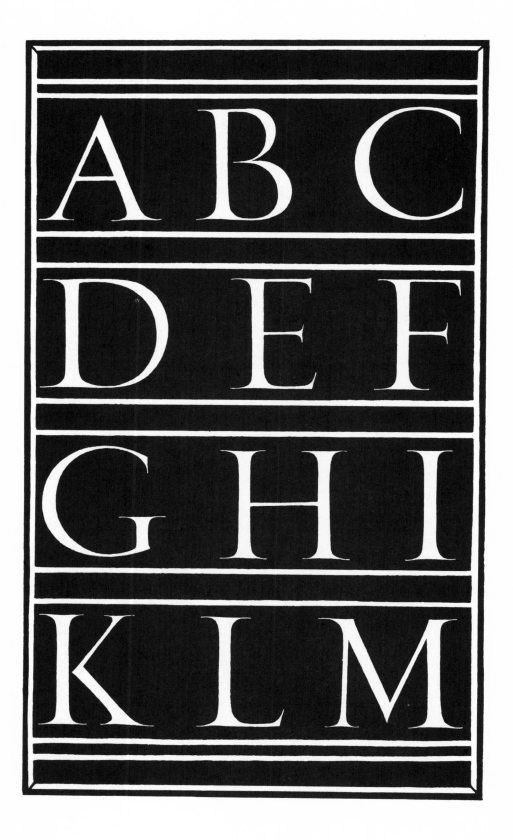

82

NOP
QRS
TVX
YYZ

83

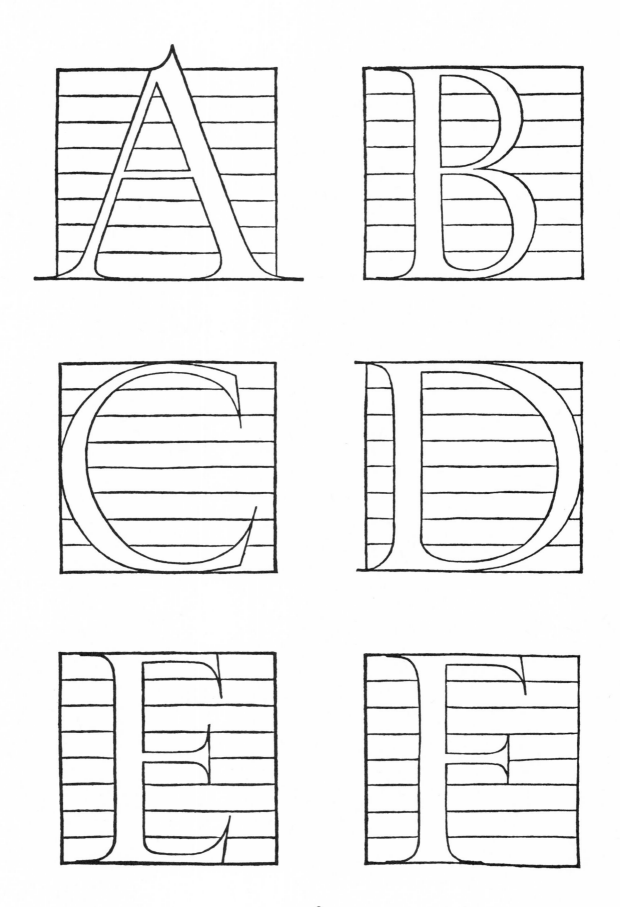

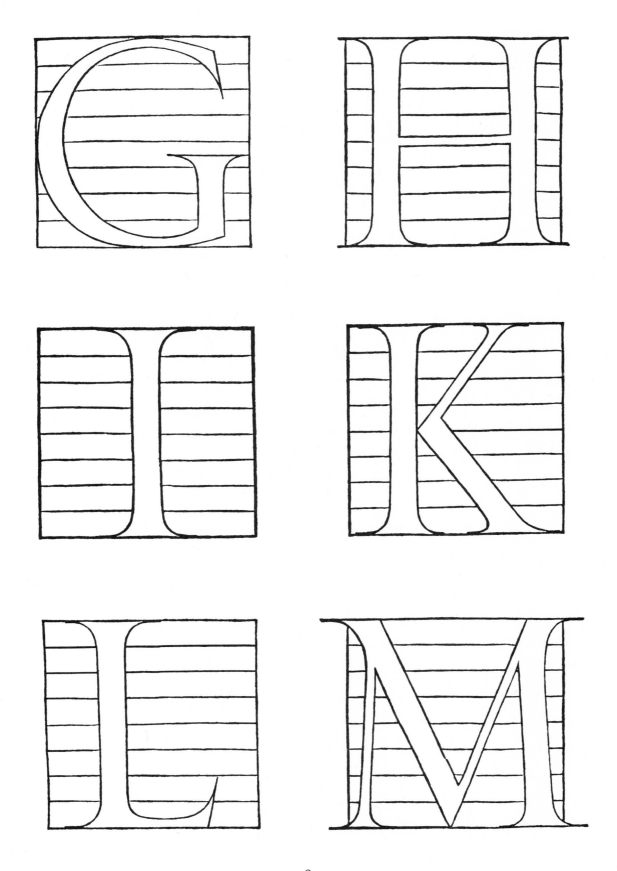

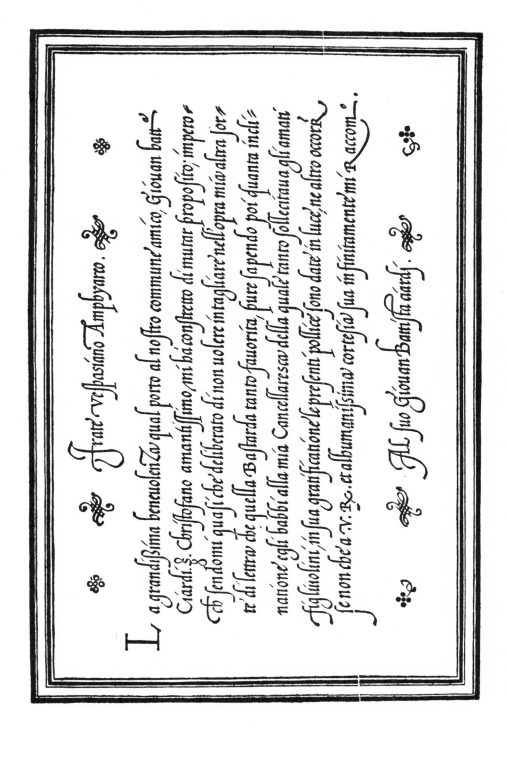

Frate Vespasiano Amphiareo

La grandissima beneuolentia qual porto al nostro commune amico, Giouan batt
Ciardi.s. Christofano amantissimo, mi ha constretto di mutar proposito, impero
ch sendomi quasi che deliberato di non uolere intagliare nell'opra mia altra sor=
te di lettra che quella Bastarda tanto fauorita, pure sapendo poi quanta incli=
natione egli habbi alla mia Cancellaresca della quale tanto sollecitaua gli amati
figliuolini, in sua gratificatione le presenti pollice sono date in luce, ne altro occor.
se non che a.v.Ra.et a humanissima cortesia sua infinitamente mi raccom.

AL suo Giouan Batta aardi.

89

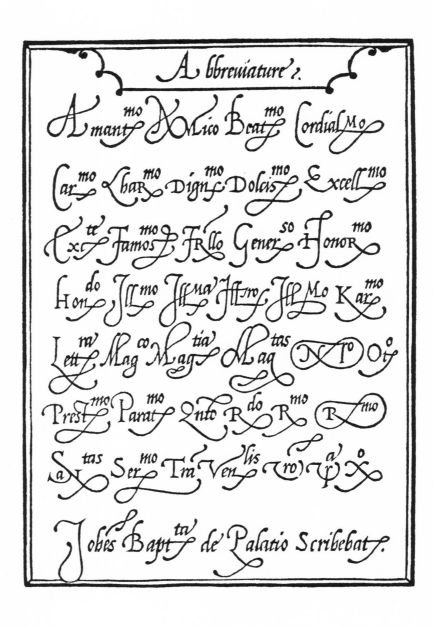

90

91

No T eniendo cosa cierta del
mundo ni de sus cosas hazemos ca
sas costosas estando el huer
co a la puerta . Se
guimos a sathanas y a ñ buen dios
no tememos de contino
te ofendemos con
los bienes que nos das .

A a b c d e f g h i k l m n o p q r .
ſs t vu x y z ꝣ .

Ioannes de yciar scribebat.
1 5 5 0
.I.D.V.

:·abc con sus principios

A·co a llfb·rc rod·eec

ll froguope g llfhh

cbb·ii llll irnm·

rn ccco ll ppp coqir

r yf ss lt vu x

vv y y 7 zzzy

Fran̄ Lucas me escre-
uia en madrid año.1570

-:- Bastarda grande llana :~

Obsecrote domina sancta

Maria mater Dei pietate

plenissima, summi regis fi-

lia, mater gloriosissima, m-

ter orphanorum, consola-

tio desolatorum, via erran-

tiuz

Fran, Lucas lo escreuia en

Madrid año de MD lxx

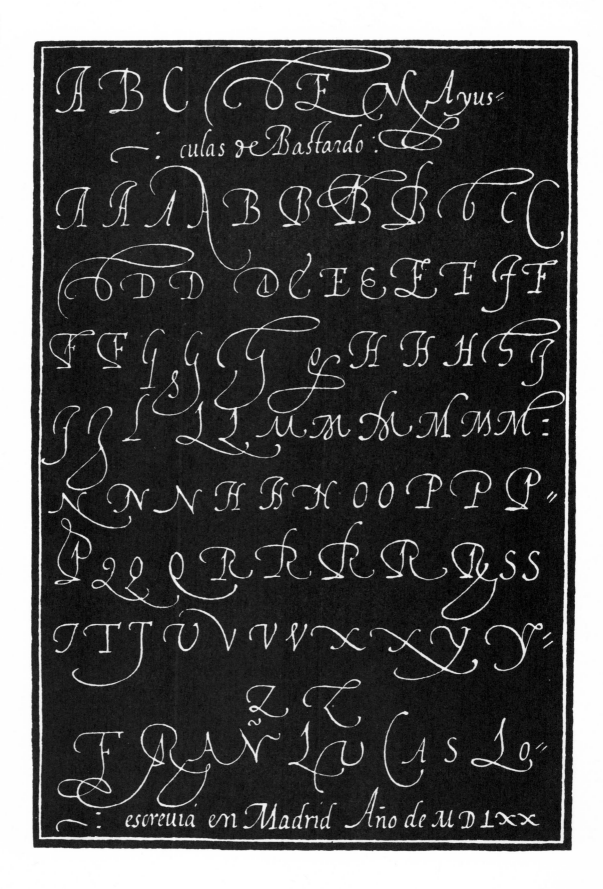

ABC DEM Ayus-

: culas de Bastardo :

escreuia en Madrid Año de MDLXX

Bastarda llana Mas peque-
~: na :~
Cantate domino canticum nouum:can
tate domino omnis terra. Cantate domi
no et benedicite nomini eius: annuntia
te de die in diem salutari eius. Annun-
tiate inter gentes gloriam eius: in omni
bus populis mirabilia eius. Quoniam
magnus dominus et laudabilis nimis:
terribilis est super omnes Deos. Quoniam omnes dij gentium dæmonia
: Dominus :~
Frañ Lucas Lo escreuia En
Madrid Año De M D lxx

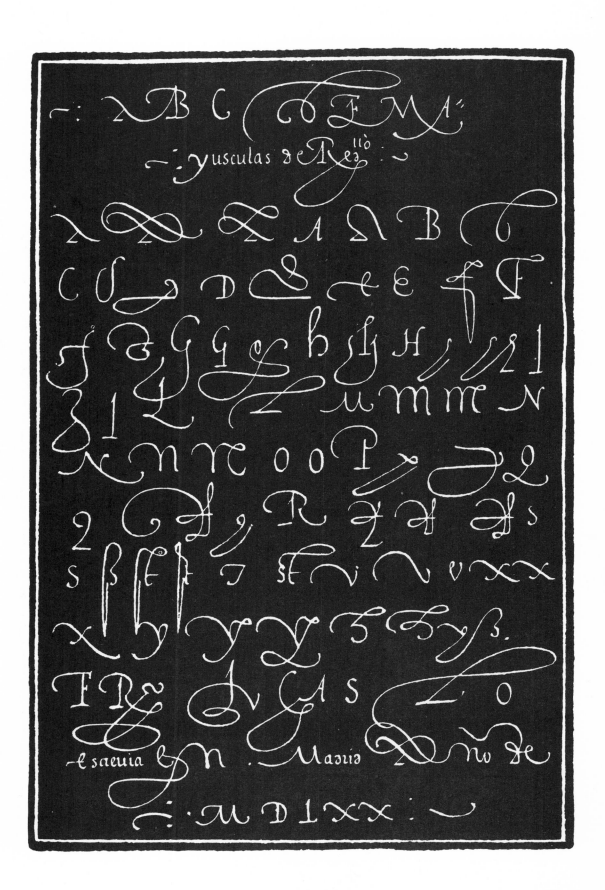

100

-: Redondilla llana mas -
-: pequena :-

La virtud es ganancia que nun
ca se pierde, rio que no se passa,
mar que no se navega, fuego que
nunca se apaga, tesoro que jamas
fenece, exercito que nunca se ven
ce, carga que nunca pesa, espia q̃
siempre buelue, guarda que no se
-: engaña :-

Frañ Lucas Lo escreuia
en Madrid Año :-
-: DE MDLXX :-

III

AFengklich vnd zum ersten von Cita-
cion: fürheischung: vnd ladung der jn
gesessenen burger in gemein.

¶ Welcher burger oder byseß einem andern jngesessnen burger oder jn woner diser statt Franckenfurt vor vnd an des heiligen reichs gericht gepieten wil/der selb sol vrsach der sachen vnd fordrung warumb/vnd wa her die erwachß/jn solchem gepot meldūg thūn/damit der antwur-ter der sachen vnd forderung wissen / vnd daruff bedacht mög haben.

¶ Vnnd sollen einem ieglichen burger drey fürgebott geschehen mit vn-derscheit wie hernach folget / Nemlichen das erste gepot persönlichen/ vnd mögen darnach die andern zwey gebott zu hauß vnd hoff gethan werden/außgescheiden für die hürige zinß/vnnd die messegebott sol ein ieglicher nach dem ersten gebott (das auch also wie obstet /in die eygen person gescheen sol)erschynē vnd antwurt zu geben/ wie von alter her kōmen ist pflichtig sein/Also doch das solche fürgebot gescheen vor dem gerichts tag bey sonnen schein/durch einen weltlichen richter zu Fran-ckenfurt. Welche gebot auch ein ieglicher richter dem gerichtschryber on allen verzug müntlichen oder schrifftlichen ansagen vnd jnschrybē las-sen so offt sich die begeben. Doch so wöllen wir soliche felle/so jnn der für heischung vnd Citation mit willen vnd erlaubung der öberkeit gesche-hen/sollen hierinn nit gezogen noch verstanden werden.

¶ Wolt sich auch einer persönlichen nit finden / oder seiner geuerlichen verleucknen lassen/so sollen vnd mögen nichts desteminder die gepott/ es weren das erst/ander/oder drit zu huß geschehen/ vnd alßdañ die sel-ben gebot crefftig geacht vnnd gehalten/vnd daruff procedirt werden.

102

Ancient Black

ABCDEFGH

abcdefghijklmnopq

JKLMNOPQ

rſstuvwxyz

RSTUWXYZ

finffnflnfffinst

Suaviter in modo,
fortiter in re

Oratio ad suu ppriu angelu.
Deus ppicius esto mihi
peccatori. Et sis mihi cu
stos omnibus diebus vite mee.
Deus Abraha. Deus Ysaac.
Deus Jacob miserere mei Et
mitte in adiutoriu meum pro
prium angelu gloriosissimu:
qui defendat me hodie: et pte
gat ab omnibus inimicis meis
Scte Mihael archangele. De
fende me in plio: vt non perea
in tremendo iuditio. Archan
gele christi. Per gratia quam

werdē/ als Hertzog Eberhard/ Keyser Conrads/ Hertzogen
zu Francken / vnd Heinrici vorfahr / Bruder / vnd vnder
andern Hertzog Arnold auß Bayern / die jhm zuvor nach
Leib vnd Leben stunden / hernach seine beste vertrauwete
Freunde worden/ vnd jn für jren Herrn vnd Röm. Keyser
erkannt vnd gehalten. Als nun dieser Heinricus in ver-
waltung seines Reichs gemeynem Teutsch vnd Vatter-
land vorzustehen allen fleyß fürwandte / alle abtrünnige
vnd widerspenstigen strafffte / die auffruhren vñ embörun-
gen/ so sich hin vñ wider erhuben/ stillete/ die vngläubigen
zum gehorsam vñ Christlichen Glauben verursachete/ vnd
darzu alle deß Reichs Fürstē jm hieriñ behülfflich zu seyn
beschriebe/ welche jren Pflichten nach erschienen / vnd das
Barbarisch Volck also bestritten/ hat er vnder andern dem
Hochgelobten Adel Teutscher Nation/ von wegen jres ge-
horsams vnd Mannlicher thaten/ zur ewigen gedechtnuß
das Ritterspiel der Thurnier/ so der zeyt bey den Teutschē
vnbekāt / aber doch in Britannia vnd anderßwo breuch-
lich/ in Teutschenlanden angefangē/ auffbracht/ auch selbs
thurnieret / vnd ferrner die vier fürnembsten Teutschen
Refier oder Kreyß/ Nemlich deß Rheinstroms/ Francken/
Bayrn vnd Schwaben / sampt andern so darinn vnd da-
runder zum Heyligen Röm. Reich Teutscher Nation ge-
hörig/ begriffen/ mit sondern Freyheiten vnd Gnaden be-
gabet/ Bey welchē hernach alle folgende Römische Keyser
vnd Könige dieselben gelassen vnd gehandhabt/ ist auch in
krafft dero ob fünff hundert vnd achtzig Jarn/ biß auff den
letzten zu Wormbs gehaltnen Thurnier/ gethurniert vnd
erhalten worden. Das aber gemeldte Thurnier zu pflan-
tzung aller ehrbarn tugenden/ Ritterlicher vbung/ Mann-

Erstlich sey vnser meynung das wir das erst beschryben angesicht durch die zwerch li=
nien gar verrucken wölle/also das kein ding bey dem andern beleyb /Eintwreders wir wöl
len ein lange oder kurtze stirn/ein lange oder kurtze nasen/ein langs oder kurtz kin machen/
Ist nun sach das du die zwerch lini.l.fast obersich ruckest gegen der lini.k.so wirdet dar=
zwischen ein kurtze stirn/vnd die nasen erlengt sich zwischen.l.m.ruckstu aber die lini.l.vn
dersich gegen der lini.m.so wirdt dir ein lange stirn zwischen.k.l.vnd ein kurtze nasen zwi=
schen.l.m. Ist aber sach das du die lini.l.sten lest/vnd ruckest die zwerch lini.m.obersich/so
wirdet aber ein kurtze nasen zwischen.l.m.aber mund vnd kin werde lang / wirdt aber die
lini.m.vndersich geruckt/so wirdt ein lange nasen zwischen.l.m.vnd kurtz mund vnd kin.
nun mögenn die zwo lini.k.m.weyt von einander geruckt werden /also das die lini.k.sey
nahent der lini.i.vnd die lini.m.nahet der lini.n.so beleybt darzwische die höhe des haubtz
vnd die leng des mundes mit sambt dem kin kurtz/aber die stirn vñ nasen fast lang. Weñ
du aber die zwo zwerch lini.k.m.nahent zusamē rukest/so wirdt die höhe des haubtes lang
des gleychen mund vnd kin/aber die stirn vñ nasen werden fast kurtz. Ruckest du.k.l.hoch
obersich/so wirdt dir ein kurtz haubt vnd ein kurtze stirn.Darnach teyl zwischen.l.n.die an
dern zwerch linien durch den verkerer gleych wider eyn/so wirdt ein lang nasen/mund vñ
kin / Dem magstu gleych vmbkert widerwerdig than / so wirdt dir ein hoch haubt vnnd
lang stirn/vnd ein kutz nasen/mund vñ kin. Aber ein andre verruckung/ruck die lini.k.na=
hent der lini.i.vnd die lini.m.nahet der lini.l.vnd laß die lini.l.sten/darauß wirdt ein nider
haubt ein lang stirn ein kurtze nasen vnd lang lebs vnd kin. Thu disem widerwerdig/ruck
die lini.k.nahent der lini.l.vnd die lini.m.nahent zu der lini.n.so wirdt ein hoch haubt ein
kurtz stirn/ ein lang nasen/kurtz mund vnnd kin. In solchem wer vil anzuzeygen/das hie
vmb kurtz willen vnderlassen ist/ auch ist in disem geben vnd nemen zu mercken das man
die linen also ruck/das man die natur nit zu vil nöttig auff das es menschlich bleyb/weli=
cher anderst solch ding ins werck zihen wil/vnd wie du mit den dreyen linien.k.l.m.gehan=
delt hast/also magstu than mit den andern zwerch linien.o.p.q.r.s.so nun nach vnsern wil
len durch die zwerch linien lang vnnd kurtz zu machen wie wirß fürnemen geteylt ist vnd
die ding anderst werde in der ersten fürgenumen vierung/doch in bar linien weyß/so mag
man die selben all ober ort zihen forn obersich hinden vndersich/vnd widerumb/oder eins
teyls etlich gerad lassen die andern krum machen. Man mag auch die forbeschrybnen ort
lini des ersten haubtz bey der nasen verrucken wie man wil/man mag auch die gestrackten
linien brechen/obersich oder vndersich/aber in den auffrechten fürsich oder hindersich/des
gleychen thut man mit den ort linien. In etlichen teyln magstu die linien wendenn wo du
hin wilt / du magst auch die felt zwischen den zwerch linien/in welchen teyln sie gebrochen
werden schiben fürsich oder hindersich / obersich oder vndersich /ein yetlicher würt im ge=
brauch finden wo von ich red.

Das du aber verstest was ich ein gebrochne lini neñ/so merck mich also/Ein fürgebne
lini sey.a.b.in die setz ein puncten.c.wo du hin wild/in dem brich sie von einander/ruck den
halb teyl obersich oder vndersich/oder setz auff die for bemelten lini zwen puncten/als da ist
.c.d.Das selb stück.c.d.brich herauß obersich oder vndersich/Des gleichen ist zu brechen auß
den auffrechten linien fürsich oder hindersich/also auch in ort linien/Darumm wil ich sagen
wie man in der enderung des angesichts die ort lini gebrochen brauche wirdet / Doch sich
for hie vnden in der figur auffgerissen die gebrochen lini/dauon oben gesprochen/vnd dar=
nach auffgerissen die negst ob beschribnen verkerten angesicht.

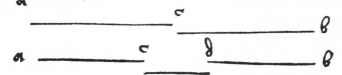

Dem Allerdurchleuchtigisten grosmechtigisten
fürsten vnd herren, herren Maximilian erwelte
Romischen Kayser vnd haubt der cristanhait auch
über cristenlicher kunigreich kung vnd ertz Ertz-
hertzogen zu Osterreich hertzogen zu Burgund etc vn
ander mechtigen fürstenthumben vnd lande in
Europa etc zu lob vnd ewiger gedachtnus seiner er-
lichen regirung lautmütigen grosmütigkait vn
siglich vberwindungen Ist dise poeten der eere mit
seinen etlichen thatten gepiert auffgericht

Jt gnaden / vñ Priuilegien / derhalben außgan-
gen / hat der Allerduchleüchtigist großmechtigist Fürst /
vnnd herr / herr / Maximilian von gots genaden Er-
wölter Römischer Kayser zů allen zeitten merer des
Reichs.zc. Jrer Mayestat diener Hansen Schönsperger bewilligt / vñ vergönt / das Bůch / genant
den Tewrdäck zůtrucken / damit Er seiner arbait /
kunst vnnd fleyß / dester fruchtbarer geniessen
möge / In der gestallt das Jme yemants / in
was stannds oder wesentts die seyen / solh
Bůch Tewrdannck genannt / weder mit
noch on figuren nicht nachtruckhen sollen / alles in zeyt vnd bey den penen / in
denselben Jrer Kayserlich Mayestat zc. Freyhaitten begriffen.

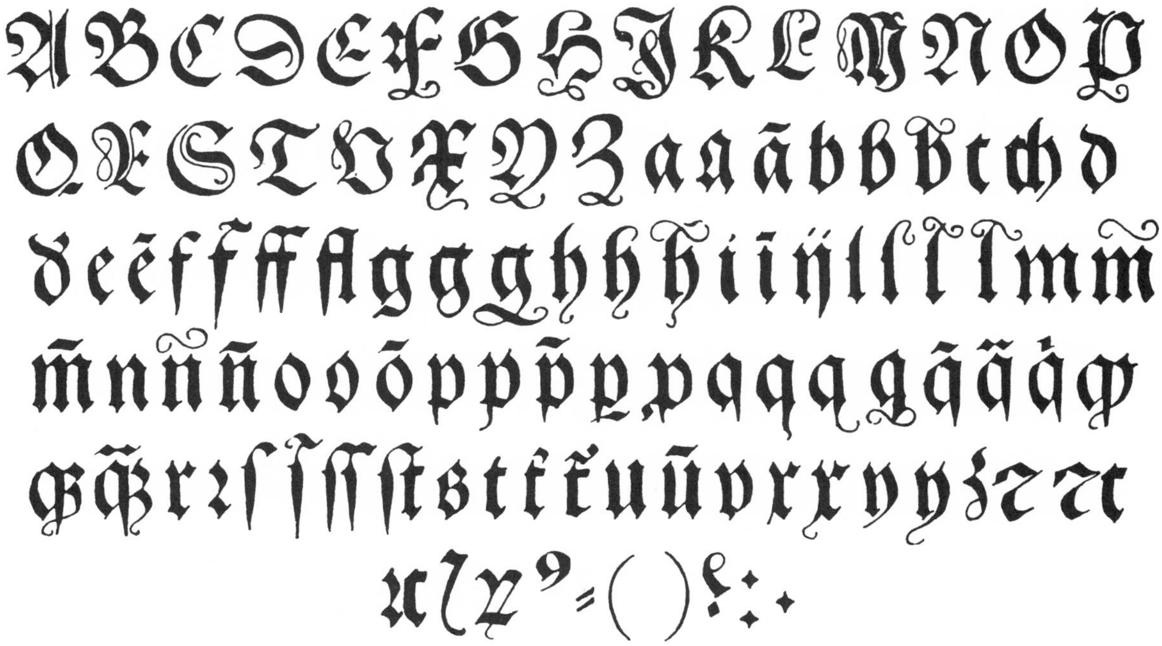

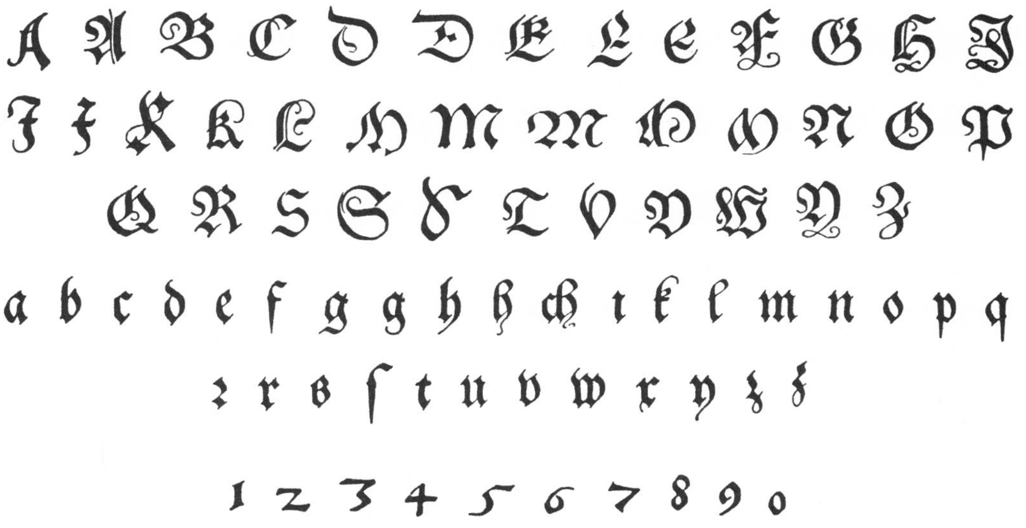

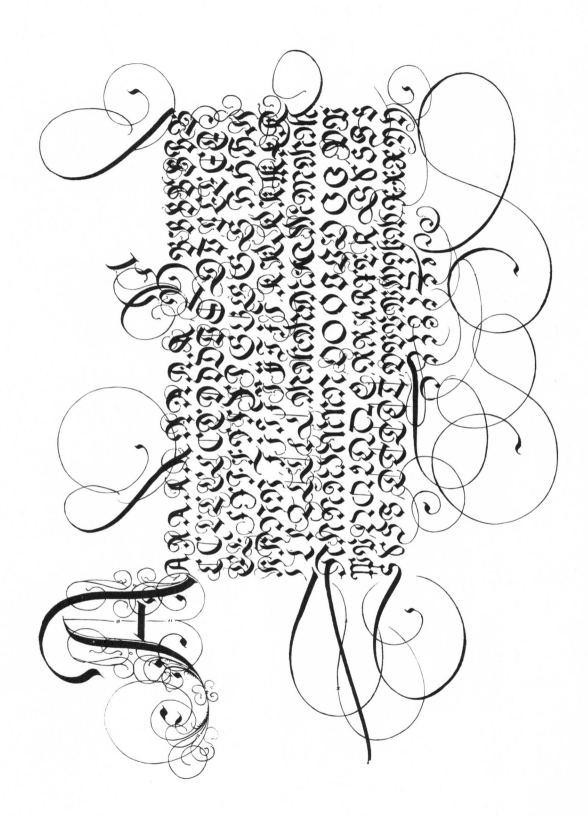

110

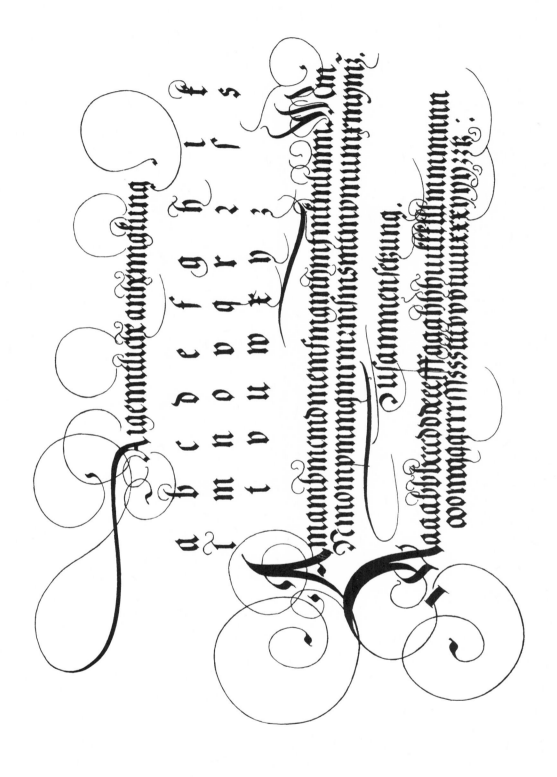

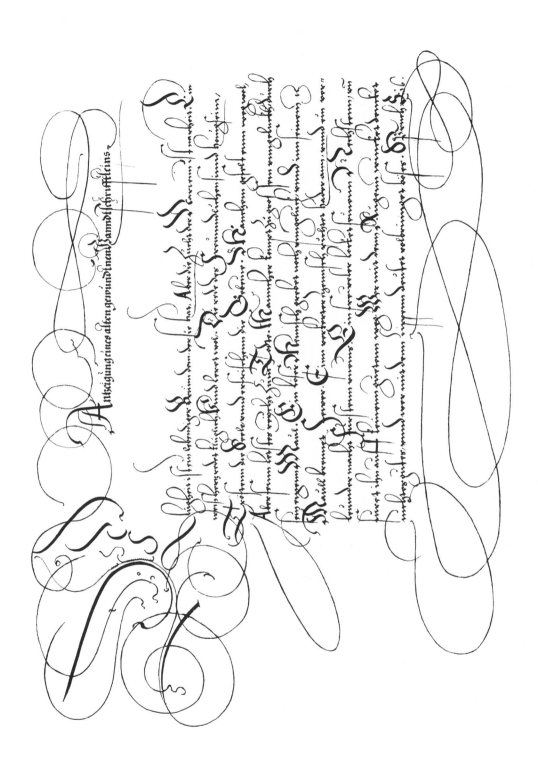

Ein jeglicher hat ein
bestimpte zeytt zu
lebē, Aber Israhels
zeyt, ist one zal. ꝗ

a b c d e f g
h i k l m n o
p q r z ſ s t
v u w x y z ❧

A B C D E F

G H I K L M

N O P Q R S

T V W X Y Z

v v, u ū ů ú, w, x, y,
z, z, ʒ, ᷓ, æ, bc bd be bg
bo bt, ce co ct, fb ff fh fk
fl fſ ft, he ho ht, œ oo œ
og œ, pp ṗp pp pe po pt, ſb
ſſ ſh ſk ſl ſſ ſt, tt tt, ve
w, we wo wo, boc bod bog

Von Pappeln. Oleander. Aron.

Spargen. Eibifch. Frawenhar.

Nachtfchatten. Tamarifck. Enifz.

Rofen. Getruckt zů Bafell/durch

Ye lenger ye lieber. Kölbleskraut.

Haselwurtz. Quendel. Weggraß.

Zeiland. Drachen. Groß. Chrift. fl

Michael Ifingrin. Latte. ff. ff. fü.

Beschreibung der Venediger Co=
nun/ Vrsprung vnd Regierung/ wie das
erwachsen / vnd bis anher erhalten
ist worden.
Durch Donatum Gianottn Florenthinern.

Der erst Dialogus.
Vnderredner.
Herr Trifon Gabriel/ Vnd Johannes Borgerinus.

Ie jenigen / so der Menschen
gebreuch zuuernemen begirig sind /
pflegen andere vnd frembde Landt
vnd Stedt zudurchziehen / zubese=
hen / vnd was sy darin̄ Jres erach=
tens theur / vnd vbertreflicher wirde
halb vnbetracht mit fürzuschreitten
befinden / vleissig zubeschreibn̄/ Auf
das Sy durch derselben erkantnus /
nit allain destaufmerckiger vnd ge=
schickter/ Sonder auch den Jenigen rais / So die Mauren Jres
Vatterlands mit lassen/ lieblich vnd fruchtbar werde.   Aus
dem kombt/ das Jr vil die gemainen vnd besonderen gepeu abne=
men: Etlich die alten Begrebnussen verzaichnen: Ander befleis=
sen sich zuerfaren / ob was theurs von disem oder Jenem Landt
herkomb: Etlich bringen beschriben/ wann Sy etwo ain Stadt/
von natur/ oder künstlicher erbawung vngewin̄lich befunden:
Ain Jeder verzaichnet das/ zudem Er von natur mer lusts hat/
Oder aber das/ welches erzelung er zum lustigisten vn̄ wunder=
lich zuhörn acht.   Von ainem solchen löblichen brauch/ hab ich
mich auch nit absöndern wellen/ Sonder beschlossen/ etwas zu
gedechtnus in̄ die schrifft zubringen/ Aus dem nit allain obge=

A 2   sagte

118

Philippe, par la grace de Dieu Roy de Castille, de Leon, d'Arragon, de Nauarre, de Naples, de Secille, de Maillorque, de Sardaine, des isles Indes, & terre ferme de la mer Oceane : Archiduc d'Austrice : Duc de Bourgoingne, de Lothiers, de Brabant, de Lembourg, de Luxembourg, de Gheldres, & de Milan : Conte de Habsbourg, de Flandres, d'Arthois, de Bourgoingne : Palatin, & de Haynnau, de Hollande, & Zeelande, de Namur, & de Zutphen : Prince de Zuaue : Marquis du sainct Empire : Seigneur de Frize, de Salins, de Malines, des cité, villes, & pays d'Vtrecht, d'Oueryssel, & Groeninge : & Dominateur en Asie, & en Afrique. A tous ceulx qui ces presentes verront salut. Receu auons l'humble supplication de nostre cher & bien amé le Docteur Benedictus Arias Montanus nostre Chappelain domestique, contenant, comme depuis enuiron quatre ans en çà, il a esté par nous enuoyé en noz pays de par de çà, auec charge & commission expresse de faire (à l'vtilité commune de la saincte Eglise Catholicque, & à la commodité de toutes personnes studieuses des sainctes lettres) bien & deuement imprimer, par Christophle Plantin nostre prototypographe, les sainctes Bibles Catholicques, és trois langues, Hebraicque, Grecque, & Latine, auec l'entiere paraphrase Chaldaicque ancienne, & les interpretations Latines du Grec, & du Chaldee, selon la copie des Bibles iadis imprimees en nostre Vniuersité de Complute en Espaigne, en y adioustant les Grammaires, Dictionaires, & autres traictez, qui pourroyent plus distinctement, commodieusement, & amplement seruir, pour plus facilement apprendre lesdictes langues, & les

Manuſkript-Gotiſch
(Old Black)

ABCDEFGHJK

abcdefghijklmnopqrſstuvwryz

LMNOPQRST

ch ck ff fi fl ll ſſ ſi ſt ßtz

UVWFYZ

äöü

Du biſt min, ich bin din:
des ſolt du gewis ſin.
Du biſt beſlozzen
in minem herzen:
verlorn iſt daz ſlüzzelin:
du muoſt och immer darinne ſin.

Schwabacher

ABCDEFGHIJKLMNOP
abcdefghijklmnopqrstuvwxyzäöüfffffffsfffsfffßstz
QRSTUVWXYZ
1234567890

———

Über die aufmachende Anemone

Der Abend war ankommen.
Ich hatte meinen Weg bereit zu ihr genommen
Zu Ihr / zu meiner Anemonen.
Ich klopfet an.
Bald ward mir aufgethan.
Die rechte Hand trug Ihr das Licht.
Die Lincke deckt ihr Angesicht.
So balde war das tiefst in meinem Hertzen
Verletzt von ihren göldnen Kertzen.
Wo kam ich hin! Sah ich denn in die Ferne!
Das kan ich itzund nicht aussprechen.
Jedoch die mir das Licht getragen /
Die war die Venus ohne Tagen
Selbselbst mit ihrem Abend=Sterne.

David Schirmer

Luthersche Fraktur

Es werden etwan vnter die Fraktur Buchstaben / einer andern schriefft Buchstaben gemengt vnnd geschrieben / als solte sie dardurch einer andern art vnd verendert sein / die sie dann warlich wol sein mag / dunckt mich / so man ein Sammate schauben mit alten hadern flicke / es sey auch ein verenderte art / derhalben man bey jrer art bleyben mag.

ABCDEFGHI
KLMNOPQRSTUVWXYZ
abcdefghijklmnopqrsßtuvwxyz
åóü chck ffstfl ll sissßst tz
1234567890

Es kumen die guten alten leßlichen Schriefften / so man vormals zutrucken gepflegt hat ytzt diser zeyt (von wegen der teglichen new geschnitnen Schriefften) schier in eine verachtung / vnd werden doch offt die newen geschnitten / wie sie mügen / yedoch wann man deren gar vergessen hat / vnnd keyn newe mer erdacht kan werden / wirt man die alten Schriefften etwan wider herfür ziehen / vnnd für new schriefften an tag geben / wie schon mit andern dingen mer geschicht.   Wolffgang Fugger 1553

123

Centaur

ABCDEFGHIKLM
NOPQRSTU
VWXYZ

abcdefghijklmnopqrst
uvwxyzäöü

1234567890

ff fi fl &

Rotunda, omnium
scripturarum nobilissima,
vocatur etiam mater
et regina aliarum

Bembo

A B C D E F G H I J K L M
N O P Q R S T U
V W X Y Z
abcdefghijklmnopqrst
uvwxyzäöü
1 2 3 4 5 & 6 7 8 9 0
ff fi fl

Antiqua, edelste der
Schriftarten, Mutter auch
und Königin genannt
aller anderen

La Sainte
Bible.
Aſtronomi
que diſcours,
Liure
extraor·

THEATRVM
Vitæ humanæ.

ABC
DEFGHIK
LMNOPQR
STVXYZ.

abcdefghijklmn
opqrſstvuxyz:
&&ᵒ﷼ff ﬆﬃ ﬁ ﬂ ﬅ
(æœ)ς ẻ ꝑ ꝓ ꝙ ꝙ̃

Garamont romain

ABCDEFGHIJKL
MNOPQRST
UVWXYZ

abcdefghijklmno
pqrſstuvwxyz
æ ff fi fl ß ſt œ

Vae qui ſapientes eſtis
in oculis veſtris

12345&67890

Garamont italique

ABCDEFGHIJKL
MNOPQRST
UVWXYZ
abcdefghijklmnopqr
ſstuvvwxyzææ
ctesfffifflfrggllſpſtſiſſiß
AuBuDuGuMuNu
PuQuRuTuUu
12345&67890

A a b c d e f g h h i j k l m n o p q r s t u x y z

T Vrbabunt gen=
tes et timebũt
qui habitant termi=
nos à signis tuis:exi=
tus   Io : Franc. Cres:

ABCDE
FGHIK
LMNOP
QRSTV
JUWXZ

Z

S'enfuit la lettre bastarde.

ous auons ceste singuliere faueur de
nature, que la vertu lance quelques traicts de
sa splendeur en l'entendement de tous : tellem^t.
que ceux qui ne la fuyuent ne laissent pas de
la voir. a b c d e f g h i l m n o p q r s t v u x y z

Il n'y a que la vertu qui soit haulte & esleuée. Elle est l'ancienne ennemie de la
tombe, la trompette de la gloire, & le fondement asseuré de la noblesse.

LVCAS SCRIPSIT.
P. ROYX SCVLPSIT.

132

ul ne deuient homme de bien à l'auenture. Il conuient aprendre la vertu. La volupté est chose vile & basse, de nul pris, commune à l'homme auec les bestes brutes, & dont les moindres & les plus contemptibles sont les plus desireuses. Quant à la gloire, c'est vn songe qui passe plus viste que le vent. La pauureté n'est mal, sinon pour celuy qui la porte impatiemment. La mort n'est point chose mauuaise. C'est elle seule qui faict iustice & se porte equitablement enuers le genre humain. Au regard de la superstition, c'est vn erreur brutal: elle craint ce quelle deuroit aimer & viole ses maistres.

133

134

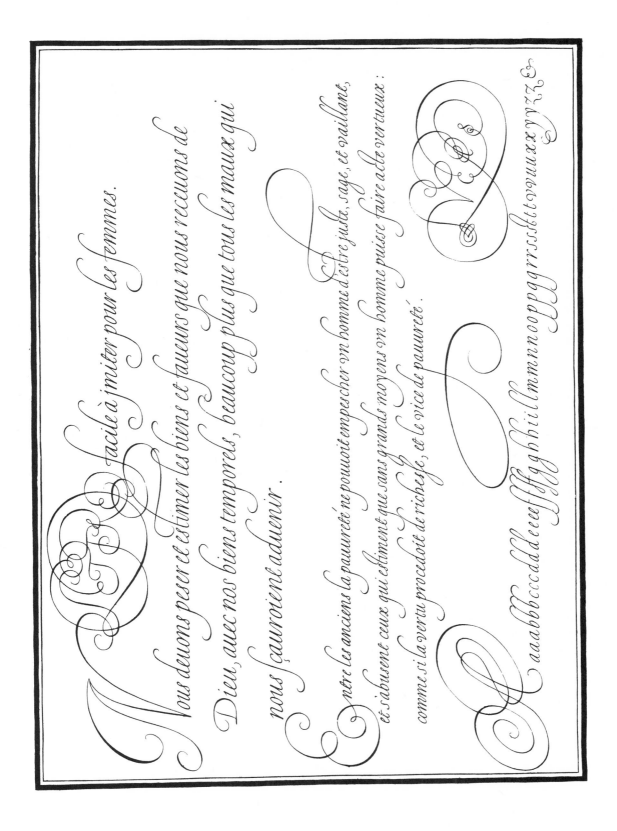

facile à imiter pour les femmes.

Nous deuons peser et estimer les biens et faueurs que nous receuons de Dieu, auec nos biens temporels, beaucoup plus que tous les maux qui nous sçauroient aduenir.

Entre les anciens la pauureté ne pouuoit empescher vn homme d'estre iuste, sage, et vaillant, et s'abusent ceux qui estiment que sans grands moyens vn homme puisse faire acte vertueux : comme si la vertu procedoit de richesse, et le vice de pauureté.

aaabbbcccdddeeefffgghhiillmmnnooppqgrrrssfttovuuxxyzz &

Super Avro

Remonstre tres-humblemen
a vre Mate la Communauté des pauures
habitans de Sct... mouv qu'en considacon
de ce qu'Ilz ont esté extraordinairemen Incommodez
par les logemens des troupes du Sr. de Rouuans Ilz
ont esté anciennen exempté de payer la subsistan.
pange quatre annexe consecutiue qui ont commenca

Lan Mil six Cens

Quavant Huict Et Septiesme

Jour de Janvier avant Midy

Pardavant Notte Vincent

de Montivault Con⟨ser⟩

du Roy et Lieutenant general en

la sarcs haulse i.

Bonnaventure Est comparu

⟨...⟩ Quentin er

vaugarillier S S. Rela

Janſon-Antiqua,
aus der Ehrhardtſchen Gieſserei,
um 1690 entſtanden

A B C D E F G H I
J K L M N O P Q R S T U
V W X Y Z Æ Œ
a b c d e f g h i j k l m n o
p q r ſ s t u v w x y z
ä ö ü . , : ; ! ? ff fi fl & ſi ſſ ſs ſt
1 2 3 4 5 6 7 8 9 0

Nach neueren Forſchungen iſt
dieſe ſchöne Schrift von Niklaus Kis,
einem Ungarn, geſchnitten worden.

Janſon-Kurſiv,
aus der Ehrhardtſchen Gießerei,
um 1690 entſtanden

A B C D E F G H I
J K L M N O P Q R S T U
V W X Y Z Æ Œ
a b c d e f g h i j k l m n o p
q r ſ s t u v w x y z
ä ö ü . , : ; ! ? ff fi fl ll & ſi ſſ ß ſt
1 2 3 4 5 6 7 8 9 0

Kis hatte den Schriftſchnitt in Holland
erlernt; ſeine Schrift entſpricht daher den
holländiſchen Lettern der Zeit.

Union Pearl
The Moſt Ancient Engliſh Types

A B C D E F F G G H I J K L M N
O P Q Qu R S T T U V W X Y Z
a b b c d e f g h h i j k l l m n o p q
r s t u v w x y z ſ ſh ſh ſt &

O for a Booke and a ſhadie nooke,
  eyther in-a-doore or out,
With the grene leaves whiſp'ring overhede,
  or the Streete cryes all about.
Where I maie Reade all at my eaſe,
  both of the Newe and Olde,
For a jollie goode Booke whereon to looke,
  is better to me than Golde.

Shelley.

143

Caslon

abcdefghijk

lmnopqrſst

uvwxyz

1234567890

ſſſſiſſ & ſſſiſſt

äô!..ß;?æø

ABCDEF

GHIJKLM

NOPQRS

TUVWXY

ÆZØ

STERNE

YORICK

Caslon's Italic

ABCDEFGHIJ
KLMNOPQ
RSTUVWXYZ
ABCDEGKM
NPRVY
abcdefghijklmnopqr
ſstuvwxyzäöüæø
hkvwffffifl&ſſſißſt
!ÆØŒ?

THE glory and power of Printing is not all in the past. Its influence in the present makes it a power-ful conservator of human progress.

It is a handmaiden of all the arts & industries, & a most effective worker in the world's workshop, to polish & refine the civil-isation of the age.

CARLYLE

147

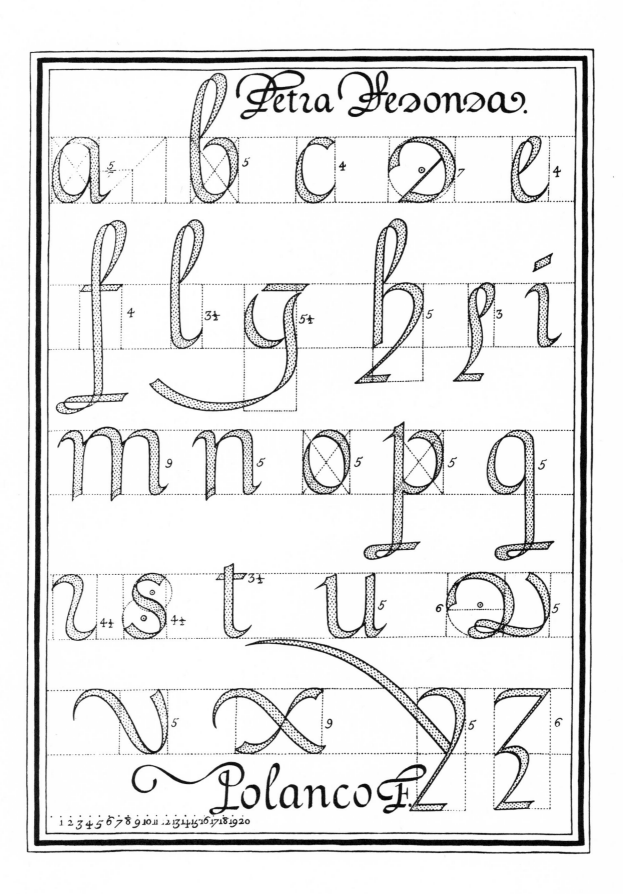

148

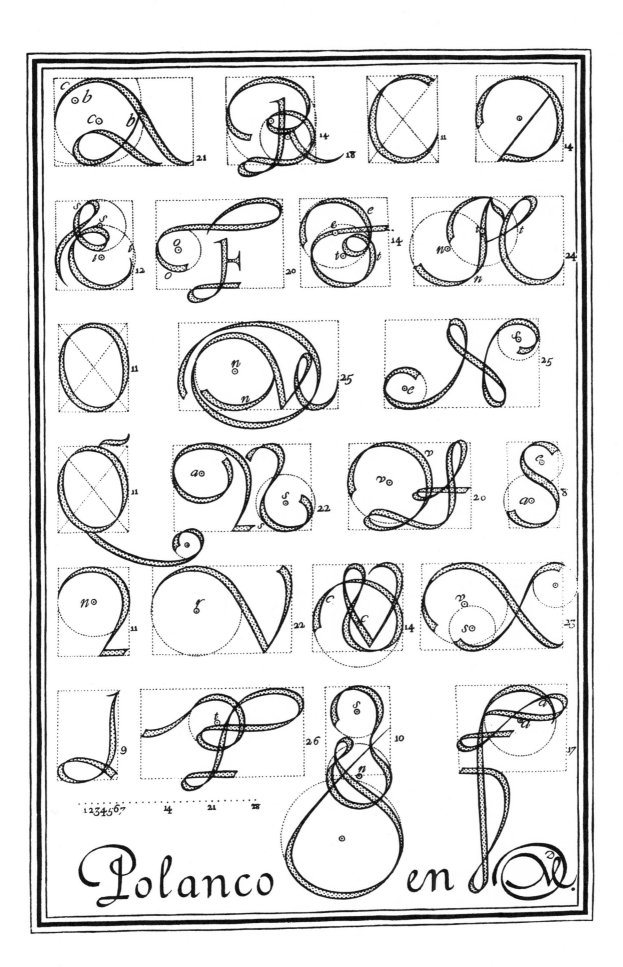

Polanco en N.

Holländische Mediäval-Antiqua
der Bundesdruckerei zu Berlin,
geschnitten von Schmidt,
wohl um 1750

A B C D E F G H I J K L M N O
P Q R S T U V W X Y Z
a b c d e f g h i j k l m n o p q r s t
u v w x y z ä ö ü
ff fi ffi ffl fl fi ffi ff fs ft
1 2 3 4 5 & 6 7 8 9 0
. , : ; ' („ § † ") ' ? ! * -

Den Geschmack kann man
nicht am Mittelgut bilden, sondern
nur am Allervorzüglichsten.
GOETHE

Holländifche Mediäval-Kurfiv
der Bundesdruckerei zu Berlin,
gefchnitten von Schmidt,
wohl um 1750

A B C D E F G H I J K L M N O
P Q R S T U V W X Y Z

a b c d e f g h i j k l m n o p q r ſ s t

u v w x y z ä ö ü

ff fi ffi ffl fl æ œ ſi ſſi ſſ ſs ſt

1 2 3 4 5 & 6 7 8 9 0

. , : ; ' („ ſ ") ' ? ! -

Ich will nicht, daſs man gänzlich
ohne Mühe leſe, was ich nicht ohne
Mühe gefchrieben habe.

Gaza frequens Libycum
duxit Kartago duxit
Karthago triumphũ
Gaza gaza frequens fre-
quens frequens frequens
duxit duxit duxit du-
xit Karthago karthago
triumphum triũphum
agagagagagagagaga
ggggggg

Gaza ffrequens Lybicū
duxit. Karthago tri-
umphum. Gaza ffrre-
quens Lybicum. ffsu
duxit Karthago hbi
triumphum. v Gaza
ufrequens lllybicum
duxit Karthago trÿ

Aa Bb Cc Dd Ee E

Ff Gg Hih Jij Kk Le

Mm Nn Oo Pp Qg

Rr Ss Tt Vuv Xxyz

as faß aß aß pa ft affr ctu

sp sti stu ac fus ss cta ctim

á é í ó ú à è ì ò ù â ê î ô û ñ cī

ōūãg̃ ë öü ç œ æ w g g g o

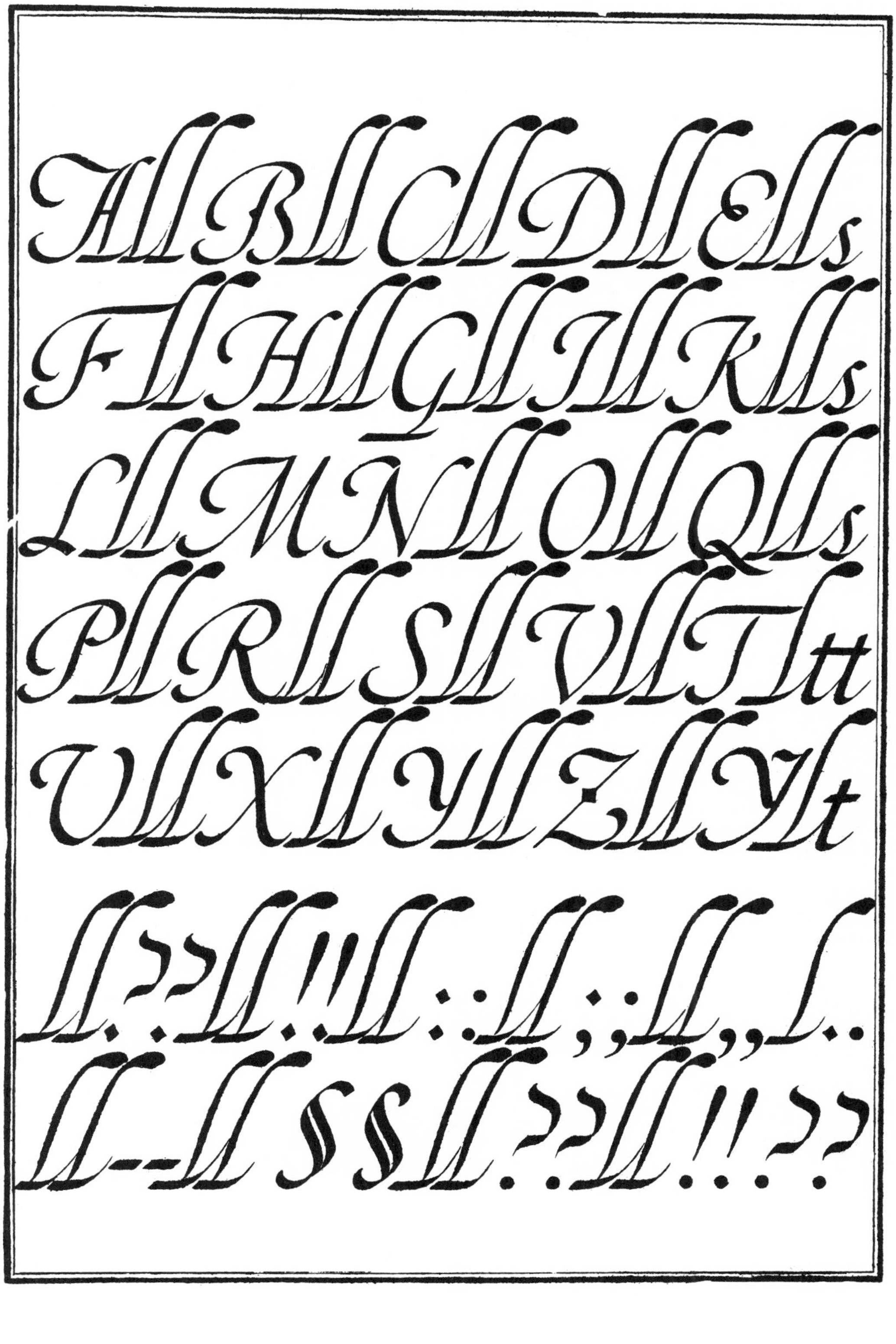
A B C D E s
F H G I K s
L M N O Q s
P R S V T tt
U X Y Z Y t

VOORBERICHT.

Reeds eenige Jaaren geleeden, heb ik ten dienste van hun, die zich door my in 't behandelen der Viool lieten onderwyzen, de tegenwoordige Regels opgesteld. Het verwonderde my menigmaal grootlyks, dat 'er tot gebruik van een zo gewoon en by de meeste Concerten byna on= ontbeerlyk Werktuig, als de Viool met der daad is, gee= ne Handleiding ten voorschyn kwam; daar men echter reeds overlang goede Grondbeginsels, en voornaamlyk eenige Regels aangaande de byzondere Strykmanier had noodig gehad. Het deed my dikwyls niet weinig leed, wanneer ik ondervond, dat de Leerlingen zo slecht onderweezen wa= ren, dat men niet alleen alles van 't begin af weder her=

* *

haalen;

JACQUES FRANÇOIS
ROSART.

MATTHIAS ROSART.

IZAAK
ET
JOHANNES
ENSCHEDE.

LA
VEUVE DECELLIER.

ABCDEFGHIJKLM   HIJLMNO   ABCDEGH

ABCDEFG   MRŒ   ABCDEFGI

ABCD   LPR   ABCDE

KŒH   YJR   FGHK

MFN   SE   JMLN

NUI   NOPRSTU

NI   GB   BLMNOPQ

FJ   IG   M M M

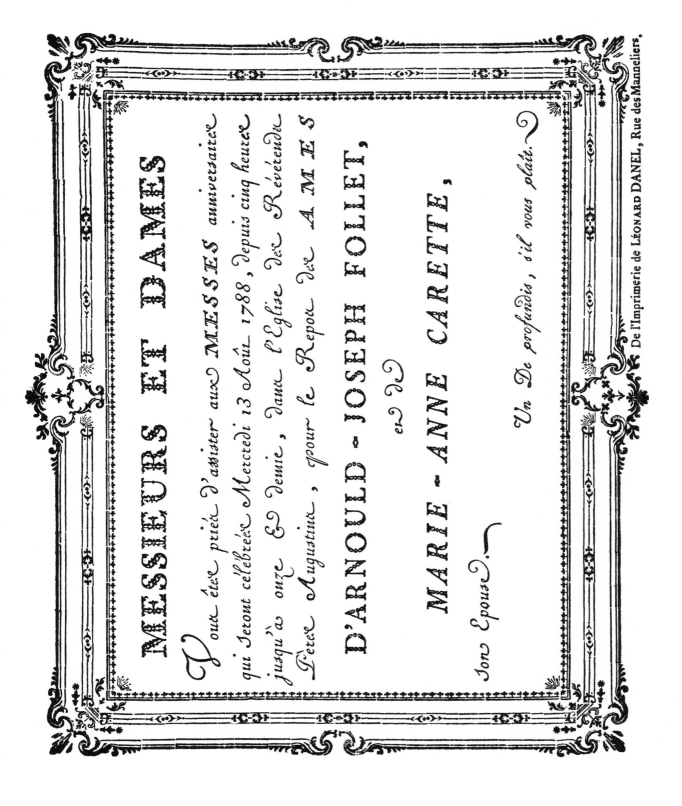

MESSIEURS ET DAMES

Vous êtes priés d'assister aux MESSES anniversaire
qui seront célébrées Mercredi 13 Août 1788, depuis cinq heures
jusqu'à onze et demie, dans l'Église des Révérends
Pères Augustins, pour le Repos des AMES

D'ARNOULD-JOSEPH FOLLET,

et

MARIE-ANNE CARETTE,

Son Épouse.

Un De profundis, s'il vous plaît.

De l'Imprimerie de LÉONARD DANEL, Rue des Manneliers.

159

The original dies of
this famous historic
design known as
Baskerville Old Face
were engraved
about 1768
£1234567890.;?!
abcdefghijklmnop
qrstuvwxyz
fifffffifl

ABCDEF
GHIJKLM
NOPQ
RSTUVW
XYZ
Æ & Œ
DRYDEN

ABCDEFGHI
JKLMNO
PQRSTUVW
XYZ

abcdefghjkmn
opqrstuvwxyz
ff ä ffi ö fl ü ffl
12345&67890
Baskerville

Baskerville Italic

ABCDE

FGHIJKLMNOPQR

STUVWXYZ

Amongst the several mechanic Arts that have engaged my attention, there is no one which I have pursued with so much steadiness and pleasure, as that of Letter-Founding. Having been an early admirer of the beauty of Letters, I became insensibly desirous of contributing to the perfection of them.

John Baskerville

abcdefghijklmnopqrs

tuvwxyzäöü

12345&67890

fffifl

Bell Roman

A B C D E F G
H I J K L M N O P Q R S T U
V W X Y Z

a b c d e f g h i j k l m n o p q r s t
u v w x y z
ä ö ü fi ff fl æ œ
1 2 3 4 5 & 6 7 8 9 0

Typography may be defined as the craft of rightly disposing printing material in accordance with specific purpose; of so arranging the letters, distributing the space and controlling the type as to aid to the maximum the reader's comprehension of the text.
Stanley Morison

Bell Italic

A B C D E F G H I J K
L M N O P Q R S T U V W X Y Z
A & V

a b c d e f g h i j k l m n o p q r s t u
v w x y z
fi ff ffi ffl fl æ œ
1 2 3 4 5 6 7 8 9 0

Typographie ist die Kunst der rechten
und dem besondern Zweck entsprechen-
den Verteilung der druckenden Elemente.
Die Buchstaben müssen gut angeordnet,
der unbedruckte Raum geschickt verteilt
und die Wirkung der Schrift geprüft
werden, damit der Leser den Text so leicht
und gut wie nur möglich aufnehmen kann.

Stanley Morison

FRY'S ORNAMENTED NUMBER TWO

BEAUTY
IS THE VISIBLE
EXPRESSION
OF MAN'S
PLEASURE IN
LABOUR

ÆCGJ&KQZŒ

OLD FACE OPEN

ABCD
EFGHIJKLMNO
PQRSTUVW
XYZ
12345&67890

NEMO
ALTERIUS SIT
QUI SUUS ESSE
POTEST

BULMER ROMAN

A B C D E F G H I J K L
M N O P Q R S T U
V W X Y Z
a b c d e f g h i j k l m n o p
q r s t u v w x y z
1 2 3 4 5 & 6 7 8 9 0
ff . , fi : ; fl ? ffi ! ffl

Eine der höchsten Tugenden
guter Typographie
ist unaufdringliche Eleganz

BULMER ITALIC

A B C D E F G H I J J K
L M N O P Q R S T
U V W X Y Z
a b c d e f g h i j k l m n o p
q r s t u v w x y z
1 2 3 4 5 & 6 7 8 9 0
ff ., fi :; fl ? ffi ! ffl

*One of the greatest virtues of
good typography
is unobtrusive elegance*

Groote Canon Duyts

ABCDE
FGHIKLMNOPQR
STUVWXYZ

1234567890

abcdefghijklmnopqrſstuvw
xyz chckffſiflſiſſßſttz äöü

Geſchnitten von

Joan Michael Fleiſchmann

in Haarlem 1748

(,:;.!?)

170

Didot-Antiqua

ABCDEFGHIJK

LMNOPQRSTU

VWXYZÆŒ

abcdefghijklmno

pqrſstuvwxyz

äöüæœ

.,!fl fi & ff ſi ſt ſs?:;

KRYSTALLINE

1234567890

DONZELLE · INCAVTE

PROLE · DISERTA

VERGINI · VERECONDE

EGRI · INDIGENTI

MARIA · LVIGIA

CONSOLATRICE · PIISS·

INVOCARONO

COMMISERANTE · VIDERO

MVNIFICA · ABBIANO

PARMA
CO' TIPI BODONIANI
MDCCCXVI.

BODONI

ABCDEF
GHIKLMN

Wenn man die Schriften Bodonis ansieht, bestaunt man diese Meister-
schaft einer so apart spezialisierten Phantasie; dieser Mann hat mit
dem Mittel der Buchstabenformen gesungen, geflötet, getanzt und
gebaut! Nicht nur als Schriftschneider war er groß, sondern ebenso
als Drucker. *Er ist der eigentliche Begründer des Begriffes vom schönen*
Buch für die neuere Zeit, des Buches, das seine Schönheit nicht dem
Schmuck, den Bildern, dem Material der Einbände, dem Aufwand an
Gold verdankt, sondern rein der Würde und dem Reiz vollendeter
handwerklicher Leistung. Hermann Hesse

OPQRSTU
VWXYZ

1234567890

BODONI-ANTIQUA

A B C D E F G H I J K L
M N O P Q R S T U
V W X Y Z
a b c d e f g h i j k l m n o p
q r s t u v w x y z
1 2 3 4 5 & 6 7 8 9 0
ff ä fi ö fl ü ft

Keine Kunst hat
mehr Berechtigung, ihren Blick auf
die künftigen Jahrhunderte zu
richten als die Typographie.

BODONI-KURSIV

A B C D E F G H I J K L

M N O P Q R S T U

V W X Y Z

a b c d e f g h i j k l m n o p

q r s t u v w x y z

1 2 3 4 5 & 6 7 8 9 0

ff ä fi ö fl ü ft

Denn was sie heute schafft,
kommt der Nachwelt nicht weniger
zugute als den lebenden Geschlechtern.
Giambattista Bodoni

Firmin Didot

A B C D E F G H I J
K L M N O P Q R S
T U V W X Y Z
a b c d e f g h i j k l m n o
p q r s t u v w x y z
1 2 3 4 5 6 7 8 9 0
fi & fl
Imprimerie

A B C D E
F G H I J K
L M N O P
Q R S T U
V W X Y Z
N O I R

Unger-Fraktur

ABCDEFGH JKLMNOPQRSTU VWXYZ

abcdefghijklmnopqrstu wxyz äöü

([.,:;ch ck ff fi fl fi ff ß ft ß -?'!])

1234567890

Ich muß freimütig bekennen, daß nur die große Vorliebe für
meine Kunst mich bei den vielen, oft undankbaren, Arbeiten tätig
erhält. Aufmunterung durch meine Landsleute, besonders durch
meine Kunstgenossen, tut es wahrlich nicht, deren oft nieder-
schlagende Urteile viel eher allen Antrieb zu diesen Versuchen
in mir zu ersticken vermögen. Indes sollen mich häufige, schon
erfahrne, Widerwärtigkeiten nicht abhalten, alle meine Kräfte
zur Vervollkommnung der Buchdruckerkunst anzuwenden.

Johann Friedrich Unger

Walbaum-Fraktur

U B C D E F G H J

K L M N O P Q R S T U

V W X Y Z

a b c d e f g h i j k l m n o p q

r s t u v w x y z ä ö ü

(. , : ; ch ck ff fi fl ll fi ff ß st tz ? ' !)

1 2 3 4 5 6 7 8 9 0

Keine Kunst braucht zur Vollendung mehr Liebe als die Kunst
der Letter, keine mehr Innerlichkeit und mehr Demut. Sie selbst
denkt nicht ans Strahlen. Das unsichtbar Geistige soll leuch=
ten. Die Wortwunder der Dichter und Weisen werden durch sie
lebendig und geben ab von ihrem Mut, ihrem Märchenglanze,
ihrer Wahrhaftigkeit und Kraft jedem, der will.

Christian Heinrich Kleukens

ABCDEFGHIJK
LMNOPQRST
UVWXYZ

A quick brown fox
jumps over the
lazy dog

12345 & 67890

(æœ.;!?fi ff fl ä ö ü)

JEAN PAUL

WALBAUM-KURSIV

ABCDEFGHIJKLMNOP QRSTUVWXYZ

Wenn Sie wüßten, wie roh selbst gebildete Menschen sich gegen die schätzbarsten Kunstwerke verhalten, Sie würden mir verzeihen, wenn ich die meinigen nicht unter die Menge bringen mag. Ohne daran zu denken, daß man ein großes Blatt mit zwei Händen anfassen müsse, greifen sie mit einer Hand nach einem unschätzbaren Kupferstich, einer unersetzlichen Zeichnung, wie ein anmaßlicher Politiker eine Zeitung faßt und durch das Zerknittern des Papiers schon im voraus sein Urteil über die Weltbegebenheiten zu erkennen gibt. Niemand denkt daran, daß wenn nur zwanzig Menschen mit einem Kunstwerke hintereinander ebenso verführen, der einundzwanzigste nicht mehr viel daran zu sehen hätte.   (Goethe in den Wahlverwandtschaften)

abcdefghijklmnopqrstuvwxyz
1 2 3 4 5 œ & œ 6 7 8 9 0
(.;!?fiffflåöü)

Gras Vibert

ABCDEFGHI
JKLMNOPQ
RSTUWXYZ
abcdefghijklmn
opqrstuvwxyz
1234567890

Romain

Gras Vibert

ABCDEFGHI
JKLMNOPQR
STUVWXYZ
abcdefghijklmno
pqrstuvwxyz
1234567890
et italique

ABCDEFGH
IJKLMNOPQRS
TUVWXYZ
1234567890
:;ÆŒ!?

PENS MAY BLOT
BUT THEY CANNOT
BLUSH

SOIERIES, SCHALS, NOUVEAUTÉS,
PERSES MOUSSELINES ET DAMAS.

G. JUILLARD

PLACE GUTENBERG   N° 3,   STRASBOURG.

THORNE SHADED

A B C D
E F G H I J K
L M N O P
Q R S T U V
X Y Z

1 2 3 4 5 & 6 7 8 9 0

ENGRAVED PROBABLY
ABOUT 1810

Thorowgood Italic

ABCDE

FGHIJKLM

NOPQR

STUVWXYZ

AMNVWY

abcde

fghijklmnopqr

stuvwxyz

fiffffl

ABCDE

FGHIJK

LMNO

PQRSTU

VWXYZ

12&34

567890

INITIALES

NORMANDES

LARGES

ABCDEF

GHIJKLM

NOPQRS

TUVWXYZ

3456790

1828

189

Lettres ombrées ornées

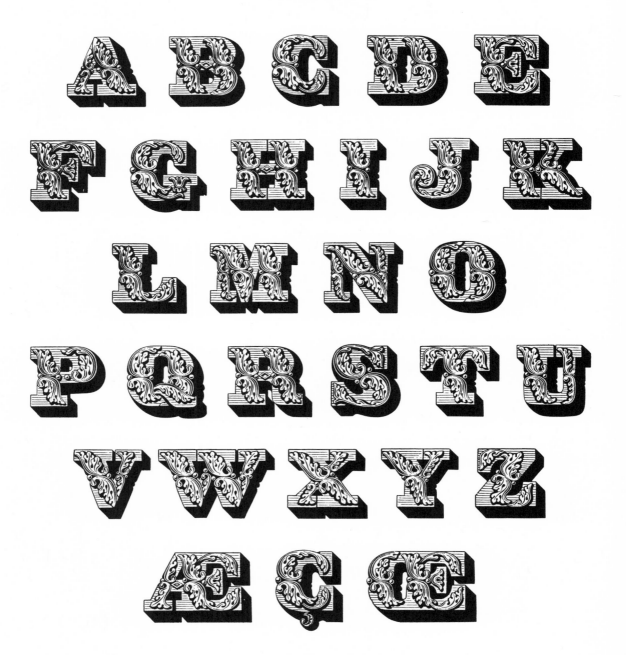

Du fonds de Gillé 1820

ROMANTIQUES

ABCDEF
GHIJKLM
NOPQRST
UVWXYZ
1234567890

ABCDEFGHI
JKLMNOPQRSTUVWXYZ
1234567890

ABCDEFGHI
JKLMNOPQRS
TUVWXYZ
abcdefghijklmn
opqrstuvwxyz
1234567889
L'avenir commence
à l'instant

ABCDEFG
HIJKLMNOP
QRSTUVW
XYZ
abcdefghijk
lmnopqrstu
vwxyz
1234567890
DAUMIER

ABCDEFGHIJ
KLMNOPQRSTU
VWXYZ
abcdefghijkl
mnopqrstuvwxyz
1234567890

A force d'étudier les vieilles choses,
on comprend les nouvelles

ABCDEFG
HIJKLMNO
PQRSTUV
WXYZ
abcdefghijk
lmnopqrstu
vwxyz
1234567890

Qui poursuit de petits avantages,
néglige les grandes choses

M M M M

HOME

LOTTERY

MEDICINE

BRIGHTON

MAMA

GREAT BRITAIN

CHESTERFIELD

PLAYBILL

ABCDEFGHIJKL

MNOPQRST

UVWXYZ

1 2 3 4 5 & 6 7 8 9 0

abcdefghijklmnop

qrstuvwxyz

Stephenson Blake

CONSORT LIGHT
in seven sizes, from 6 to 30pt

• • ◆ • •

A B C D E F G H I
J K L M N O P Q R S T
U V W X Y Z
A quick brown fox
jumps over the lazy dog
æ (.,:;' fifffl Æ & Œ ffiffl -!?] œ
I pack my box with
five dozen liquor jugs
1 2 3 4 5 6 7 8 9 0
This is 30 point

• • ◆ • •

STEPHENSON BLAKE
SHEFFIELD AND LONDON

Clarendon

ABCDEFGHI
abcdefghijklm
JKLMNOPQR
nopqrstuvwxyz
STUVWXYZ
æ & œ ø fi fl ß
Æ Ø Œ
HORA FUGIT
1234567890

Taille-douce

A B C D E F G H I
J K L M N O
P Q R S T U V W
X Y Z

a b c d e f g h i j k l m n o p q r r
s t k u v w x y z

1 2 3 4 5 & 6 7 8 9 0

Der Mensch ist ein Federvieh,
denn gar mancher zeigt, wie er a Feder
in d'Hand nimmt, dass er ein Vieh ist.

Nestroy

A B C D E

F G H I J K

L M N

O P Q R S T U

V W X Y Z &

abcdefghyklmnopqrstuvwxyzz

Französische Grotesk

ABCDEFGHIJKLM
NOPQRSTUV
WXYZ

1234567890

abcdefghijklmnopqr
stuvwxyz&äöü

Von Kindheit an hatte
ich eine Vorliebe fürs Lesen,
und das wenige Geld, das in
meine Hände kam, legte
ich durchaus in Büchern an.

Benjamin Franklin

Kompakte Grotesk

ABCDEFGHIJKLM NOPQRSTUV WXYZ

1234567890

abcdefghijklmnopq rstuvwxyz&äöü

Bücher sind kein Spielzeug für mich, sondern Handwerksgeräte, gehören zu meines Lebens Nahrung und Notdurft.

Johann Georg Hamann

Gill Sans

ABCDEFHIJ
KLMNOPQR
TUVWXYZ
1234567890
abcdefghi
jklmnopqrstu
vwxyz&

ABCDE
FGHIJKL
MNO
PQRSTU
VWXYZ
SANS

Perpetua Roman

ABCDEFGHI
JKLMNOPQRST
UVWXYZ
abcdefghijklmnop
qrstuvwxyz
12345&67890
ffäfiöfl

Langsame Arbeit
schafft feine Ware

Perpetua Italic

ABCDEFGHI
JKLMNOPQRST
UVWXYZ

abcdefghijklmnopq
rstuvwxyz

12345 & 67890

fi ff fl ffi ffl

Ein Weiser lernt selbst
von den Reden der Toren

Weiß-Antiqua

ABCDEFGHIJKLM
NOPQRSTUV
WXYZ

abcdefghijklmnopqrst
uvwxyzäöü
chck ct et & ff fi fl ft ß
1234567890

The essential qualities of
Lettering are legibility, beauty,
and character.
Edward Johnston

Weiß-Kursiv

A A B C D E F G H I J K L
M N O P Q Qu R S T U V
W W X Y Z Th

a b c d e f g h i j k l m n o p q r s t
u v w x y z ä ö ü
ch ck ct et ff fi fl ft ß st & e m n t
1 2 3 4 5 6 7 8 9 0

Die wesentlichen Eigenschaften
guter Schrift sind
Leserlichkeit, Schönheit und Eigenart.
Edward Johnston

ABCDEF
GHIJKLMN
OPQRST
UVWXYZ
SCIRE
NOSTRVM
REMINISCI

WEISS-KAPITALE MAGER

210

ABCDEE
FGHIJKLMN
OPQRSTU
VWXYZ
LEGENDO
·ET·
SCRIBENDO

WEISS-LAPIDAR MAGER

Graphik

A B C D E F G H
F K L M N O P Q R S
T U V W X Y Z

abcdefghijklmnopq
rstuvwxyz
äöüchckffllßtz&.,-;!?
1234567890

Frisch begonnen,
halb gewonnen

GRAPHIQUE

ABCDEFGHIJ

KLMNOPQRS

TUVWXYZ

1234567890

EIDENBENZ

213

ABCDEFGHI
JKLMNOPQRSTU
VWXYZ

abcdefghijklmno
pqrstuvwxyz
([.,:;«åffäfiöftüßø»?'!])
12345 æ & œ 67890

Satz ohne Einzüge ist undeutlich.
Einzüge helfen dem Leser und sichern
für immer die Ordnung des Textes.

JAN TSCHICHOLD

ABCDEFGHIJKL
MNOPQRSTUVWXYZ
abcdefghijklmnopqrstuvwxyz
12345 & 67890

Une composition sans rentrées nuit à la clarté du texte.
Les renfoncements aident le lecteur et, seuls,
garantissent pour toujours l'ordre voulu du texte.

———

ABCDEFGHIJKL
MNOPQRSTUVWXYZ
abcdefghijklmnopqrstuvwxyz
12345 & 67890

Flush paragraphs reduce clarity
Indentations are the reader's aid and alone ensure
correct division of the text for all time.

UNIVERS 55

ABCDEFGHIJK
LMNOPQRSTU
VWXYZ
abcdefghijkl
mnopqrstuvwxyz
12345&67890

Quum chartae
maxime usu humanitas
vitae constet et memoria
PLINIUS

UNIVERS 65

ABCDEFGHIJK
LMNOPQRSTU
VWXYZ
abcdefghijklm
nopqrstuvwxyz
12345 & 67890

Papier hütet
die Zivilisation und
die Erinnerung an das
Vergangene

Minerva Roman

A B C D E F G H I J K L
M N O P Q R S T U V W
X Y Z

abcdefghijklmnopqrst
uvwxyz
fi ff fl & ffi ffl
12345 , . : ; ! ? 67890

The world's simplest and most ancient letterpress print was the fingerprint. Its unmistakable individuality was known in China long before the Christian era.

Minerva Italic

A B C D E F G H I J K L
M N O P Q R S T U V W
X Y Z

abcdefghijklmnopqrst
uvwxyz
&
12345 , . : ; ! ? 67890

L'épreuve typographique la plus
ancienne et la plus simple du monde
est l'empreinte du doigt encré.
Son caractère individuel était connu
en Chine bien avant notre ère.

Antiqua, Urbild
unsrer Druckschrift
inmhulocdqeapb
rsgfffftttvwxy
.,:: jzkß -!?
1234567890
ILHEFTUOCQGD
SJPBRKNMVW
AXYZ

A drama gain many want tailor

eat neck eject member ease see creep

mile lion mind pine hive iris vivid

none home moan loam droop does

used turn just fun suit upon future

anniversary banister counterpane

dictionary excitement firmament

garment handwriting invitation

journey kindness leader manner

navigation operator perambulator

quarter recitation sunshine trees

under vinegar winding yesterday

Eastbourne Exeter Faversham Hove

Ipswich Lowestoft London Torquay

Aldershot Kidderminster Maldon

Newbury Nuneaton Windsor York

Croydon Gillingham Oxford Dover

Penzance Bolton Rochdale Saltash

Amazon Borneo Canada Denmark

Egypt France Gemini Holland Iraq

Jupiter Kiel Latvia Mediterranean

Niagara Ohio Popocatepetl Quebec

Russia Sweden Tasmania Uranus

Vesuvius Wales Yangtse Zambesi

COLUMNA
VERSALIEN

—

ABCDE
FGHIJKLM
NOPQ
RSTUVW
XYZ

ROMULUS
KAPITALEN

—

ABCDE
FGHIJKLM
NOPQ
RSTUVW
XYZ

Romanee Romein & Open Kapitalen by Jan van Krimpen,
Joh. Enschedé en Zonen, Haarlem

A B C D E F G H I J K L M N O P Q R S T U V W X Y Z .

A FONT OF TYPE

The latent mine—these unlaunch'd voices—passionate powers,
Wrath, argument, or praise or comic leer or prayer devout,
(Not nonpareil, brevier, bourgeois, long primer merely)
These ocean waves arousable to fury and to death,
Or sooth'd to ease and sheeny sun and sleep,
Within the pallid slivers slumbering.

WALT WHITMAN · 1888

A B C D E F G H I J K L M N O P Q R S T U V W X Y Z

NOTES ON THE PLATES

INDEX

NOTES ON THE PLATES

49. *Capitalis Romana*. Gravestone of a flute player, first century A. D., Cologne, Wallraf Richartz-Museum. Beautiful example of a simple, yet careful arrangement. To avoid monotony, the stonecutter made the letters in the first line larger than in the following lines.

50 and 51. *Capitalis Romana*. Part of the inscription on the Trajan Column, Rome, 114 A. D. The inscription is on a rectangular panel. It is slightly above the gate located at the base of the high, round column which is adorned with figural reliefs spiraling around it. The inscription is justly known as the most beautiful of all Roman letters. It can be regarded as the best basic form in the evolution of our letters. We should study and admire the great beauty of the individual letters, and also the rhythm of their relationship. Observe the distances between the letters – unusual and strong as they may seem to some of us – and take them as a guide. The top line is approximately 6 feet above eye-level. The upper lines were therefore kept larger than the lower ones, in order to achieve the impression of uniform line height. The letters of the upper lines stand about 4½ inches.

52 and 53. *Capitalis Romana*. Here we have an alphabet carefully copied from that in the inscription of the Trajan Column. I have outlined suitable forms for the missing letters. The Romans did not use J, U, W, and rarely used Z, H and K. The variation in the strokes indicates that the letters were first drawn on the stone with a broad stroke brush since there are no technical reasons whatsoever to explain the alternation of thick and thin strokes in letters cut in stone with a chisel.

54a. *Capitalis Quadrata*. Virgil, Georgica. Vatican, Vat. lat. 3256 (Codex Augusteus). Actual size. A straight pen stroke which is less formal than the Trajan letters, but of similarly majestic appearance.

54b. *Capitalis Quadrata*. Virgil, Georgica. 4th century A.D. St. Gallen, Stiftsbibliothek, cod. 1394. Slanted pen position.

54c. *Capitalis Rustica*. Prudentius, Hymnus. 5th century A.D. Paris, Bibliothèque Nationale, cod. lat. 8084. Very slanted pen position. The script's name means, of course, rustic or pastoral, which is probably meant to convey "simple" or "primitive."

55a. *Early Roman Cursive*. From a bill written on papyrus, 167 A.D. London, P. 730.

55b. *Uncial*. 5th century, France. Vatican, Vat. lat. 7223. Actual size. The script derived its name from *uncia*, inch.

55c. *Slanted Pen Stroke Uncial*, 4th century A.D. Berlin, Ms. theol. lat. fol. 485 (Quedlinburger Itala-Fragmente). Close to actual size. This type of majuscule form received its fluidity through the rounding of the letters A, D, E, G, H, M and V.

56a. *Uncial*. Gospel according to St. Matthew. 8th century. Paris, Bibliothèque Nationale, cod. lat. 281.

Extremely form-perfected, thus very slow, script written with a straight stroke.

56b. *Later Roman Cursive*. Script of Diocletian and Maximian, on papyrus. Middle of the 4th century. Leipzig, P. 530.

56c. *Half Uncial*. 6th century, Southern Italy. Vatican, cod. lat. 3375. The name indicates that the script is partly a majuscule and partly a minuscule letter. Faster to write than the Uncial, it marks the beginning of the minuscule, or lower case letter.

57. The script of the *Book of Kells*. Irish, Anglo-Saxon half-Uncials. Probably 7th century. Dublin, Trinity College. Exact size, from the facsimile of the Book of Kells, Urs-Graf-Verlag, Bern.

58. *Carolingian Minuscule*. Around 870. Northern France. From the Second Bible of Charles II (the Bald, 823–877). Paris, Bibliothèque Nationale, cod. lat. 2.

59. *Carolingian Minuscule*. 9th to 10th century. Evangeliar of Metz. Paris, Bibliothèque Nationale, cod. lat. 9388.

60. *Uncial*. From "Gregorius Magnus Papa, Liber sacramentorum." Vienna, Nationalbibliothek, cod. 358. Gold script, gold and color frame, without full margins. Actual size. According to R. Beer's "Monumenta Palaeographica Vindobonensia," Leipzig, 1910–13.

61. *Carolingian Minuscule* with *Rustica* and "*built-up*" *capital letters* (line 3–5). Capitularium of Ansegisus. French, 9th century, after 873. Formerly in the collection of Sir Thomas Phillipps. Reduced in size.

62. *Late Carolingian Minuscule*, transition to early Gothic. Salzburgian, mid-12th century. Beginning of the gospel according to St. John, from the Perikopenbuch of St. Erentrud of Salzburg, now at the Bayrischen Staatsbibliothek (cod. lat. 15903). The Evangelist's symbol is the first letter of the first word (In principio erat verbum).

63. *Round Gothic*. Page from an English handwritten script, end of the 13th century. Quill stroke script, parchment. Gewerbemuseum Darmstadt. Close to actual size.

64. *German Textur type* from the print-shop of Albrecht Pfister, Bamberg (Beginning of the debate between the Peasant and Death by Johannes von Saaz). Around 1462. Slightly reduced. The paragraph mark, as well as both initials, are red in the original.

65. *German Textur type* from the printing office of Johann Numeister, Mainz (Johannes de Turrecremata, Meditationes), 1479. Actual size. The illustration is a metal cut. Spacing for initial (I) still empty. In early printing, the initials were drawn by hand in color.

66. The so-called *Bastarda*, a modified version of the *Schwabacher*, from Johannes Schönsperger's workshop (Aesop's Fables), 1491. Perfect harmony of type and wood-cut.

67. *Textur*. Title of the index to Hartmann Schedel's

chronicle. Nürnberg, Anton Koberger, 1493. Cut in wood according to calligraphic patterns. Actual size.

68. *Henrik Lettersnider's Textur-type.* Around 1495. Plate reproduces one page from the *Chronik von Brabant,* Antwerp, 1497 (according to Ch Enschedé, "Fonderies de Caractères...," Haarlem, 1908). Full size. The letter, a Textur of Dutch coinage, forms a tight "fabric" or "texture" which accounts for the name. This is one of the two oldest Textur-types and the plates have survived till today. They are the property of the Lettergieterij Joh. Enschede en Zonen, Haarlem.

69. *Textur.* Title page of the book "De pluribus claris etc. mulieribus" by Jacobus Philippus Bergomensis. Ferrara, Laurentius de Rubeis de Valentia. 1497. Woodcut. Somewhat reduced. Actual height of complete drawing: about 10 inches.

70. *Large German Textur-type* from the workshop of Johannes Fust and Peter Schöffer in Mainz (Psalter of 1457). Part of a page, right upper and lower side cut off. Actual size; the Lombardic capital letters are red in the original.

71. Above: A *Textur* alphabet with ligatures (joined characters) from the workshop of Konrad Kachelofen, in Leipzig, around 1495. Actual size.

71. Below: *Textur* from the workshop of Steffen Arndes in Lübeck, 1495, Actual size. The I in the middle, and the names in the second and seventh lines are red in the original.

72. *Round Gothic type* from the workshop of Konrad Stahel and Matthias Preinlein in Brüm (Hungarian chronicle), 1488. Actual size; two lines at the bottom omitted.

73. *Ornamental title page* for "Ars Moriendi ou l'Art de Bien Mourir", cut by Jean Duvet, Lyon, 1496.

74. *Humanistic Minuscule* from Cicero's "De Oratore," hand lettered 1453 in Florence by Gherardo di Giovanni del Ciriagio. Original size. From a private collection in England.

75. *Humanistic Minuscule.* Lactantius. De divinis institutionibus. Italy, 15th century. Formerly in the collection of Sir Thomas Phillipps. Slightly enlarged.

76. *Nicolas Jenson's Roman.* From Eusebius, De praeparatione evangelica, Venice. Nicolas Jenson, 1470. Full size. Type of the Venetian roman (slanted e-bar, M with upper serifs on both sides). One of the most beautiful of all roman type faces. The capital letters hark back to the chisel shapes of the ancient Romans and have serifs which flow smoothly into the vertical strokes. The lower case letters are derived from the handwritten form of the roman of the 15th century, yet – particularly in the lower serifs – were adapted to the style of the capital letters.

77. Alphabet according to *Felice Feliciano.* These letters ("Felix Titling," Monotype Series 399), existing only in a size of 72 points, were cut from an alphabet which the Veronese calligrapher Felice Feliciano developed in 1463 in a treatise on the Roman inscriptions. This, the earliest work on Roman inscriptions, has never been published. It is preserved in the Vatican Library as Vatic. lat. 6852. D and K are definiteiy too wide.

78. *Humanistic Minuscule.* Two sets of pages in original size from a small prayer book hand lettered by Marcus Vincentinus (Marcus de Cribellariis) at the end of the 15th century. From a private collection in England.

79. *Cancellaresca Corsiva.* A page from Ludovico (Arrighi) Vicentino's Ethica of Aristotle written for Vittoria Colonna in 1517. Full size. Margin shortened in upper and lower right. Amsterdam, Universiteits Bibliotheek. Photograph courtesy of Mr. H. de la Fontaine Verwey.

80. *Cancellaresca Corsiva* of Ludovico Vicentino. Two pages from his book "La operina... da imparare di scrivere littera Cancellaresca," Rome, 1522. Original size. This is the earliest and most important textbook on Cancellaresca.

81. *Cancellaresca Corsiva* of Giambattista Palatino. Two pages from his book "Libro... nel quale s'insegna a scrivere..." Rome, 1545. Original size. This textbook of writing had received numerous editions between 1540 and 1588.

82 and 83. *Roman alphabet* of Ludovico Vicentino. From his textbook "Il modo de temperare le Penne..." Venice, 1523. Enlarged and carefully retouched by the author. The height of the original woodcut is about 6 ½ inches. One of the most elegant renderings of this Italian Renaissance script.

84 through 87. *Roman alphabet* of Frate Vespasiano Amphiareo. From his textbook "Opera... nella quale s'insegna a scrivere..." Venice, 1572. Woodcuts, original size. The horizontal lines are to facilitate copying and indicate that the height of the letters is eight times that of the diameter of the main lines. Possibly the best design of such letters from the age of the Italian Renaissance.

88. *Lettera Antiqua Tonda* (Antiqua minuscules), *Cancellaresca Corsiva* and *Lettera Trattizata.* From "Libro... de lo... scrivere" by Giovanni Antonio Tagliente, Venice, 1531. The original is a woodcut, always poorly printed. In this version the author has laboriously reconstructed the intended form. Slightly enlarged. Actual height approximately 6 inches.

89. *Cancellaresca Corsiva* of Frate Vespasiano Amphiareo. From his textbook "Opera... nella quale si insegna a scrivere," Venice, 1554. Woodcut. Actual size.

90. *Abbreviature.* Another page by Palatino, 1545 (see plate 81). Original size.

91. *Ornamental Textur Minuscules* from the book "Libro nel quale s'insegna a scrivere" by Giambattista Palatino, Rome, 1545. The original is a woodcut. Actual size. A very beautiful and harmonious page.

92. *Casos peones* (Lombardic majuscules). From the book "Arte Subtilissima..." by Juan de Yciar, Saragossa, 1550. Enlarged. Height of original approximately 6 inches. Carefully retouched by the author.

93. *Cancellaresca romana* from "Arte Subtilissima" by Juan de Yciar, Saragossa, 1550. Enlarged. The origi-

nals are woodcuts and measure approximately 6 inches in height.

94 and 95. *Letra formada Redonda* (Spanish Rotunda). From "Arte Subtilissima" by Juan de Yciar, Saragossa, 1550. Enlarged. The originals are woodcuts and approximately 6 inches high.

96 and 97. *Bastarda grande llana* (Spanish italic) (dated 1570). From the book "Arte de escreuir" by Francisco Lucas, Madrid, 1577. The originals are woodcuts, frequently very badly printed and about 6 inches high. This version was enlarged and carefully retouched. Perfectly formed Spanish italics. The capitals are shown on page 98.

98. *Majuscules of Spanish italics* (Bastarda) (dated 1570). From "Arte de escreuir" by Francisco Lucas, Madrid, 1577. The original is a poorly printed woodcut, difficult to decipher, which the author was able to reproduce with much retouching and reference to several editions. It has never been published in such a clear rendering. Enlarged. Height of original about 6 inches.

99. *Bastarda llana más pequeña* (Spanish Italic dated 1570). From the book "Arte de escreuir" by Francisco Lucas, Madrid, 1577. As on page 98, enlarged and carefully retouched by the author. Original height about 6 inches.

100. *Majuscules of Redondilla* (Spanish round hand) (dated 1570). From the book "Arte de escreuir" by Francisco Lucas, Madrid, 1577. Enlarged and carefully retouched by the author. Original height about 6 inches.

101. *Redondilla llana más pequeña* (Spanish round hand) (dated 1570). From the book "Arte de escreuir" by Francisco Lucas, Madrid, 1577. Enlarged and carefully retouched by the author. Original height about 6 inches.

102. *Textur and Schwabacher*. Page from the book "Reformacion der Stat Franckenfort am Meine des heilgen Romischen Richs Camer anno 1509." Mainz, Johann Schoeffer, 1509. Actual size. Above Textur, below Schwabacher.

103. *Ancient Black*. An especially beautiful old cut which leaned – as the Manuscript Gothic (page 120) – on the French Textur scripts of the late 15th century. The cut is owned by the Stephenson, Blake & Co. type foundry in Sheffield.

104. *Earliest Fraktur-type*. Page from the "Diurnale" known as the prayer book of Emperor Maximilian I. Nürnberg, Hans Schönsperger, 1514. Type, actual size. The first line and the initial D of the second and third line are red in the original. Earliest Fraktur type, and one of the most beautiful. The complete alphabet is found on page 109.

105. *Fraktur*. Part of a text page from a "Thurnier-Buch," or book of tournaments, published in Frankfurt on Main, 1560, by Sigmund Feyerabend. Set in a font of the early and particularly beautiful Neudörffer-Andreä Fraktur that was cut in 1526. Actual size.

106. A font of the *Neudörffer-Andreä Fraktur* often erroneously called Dürer Fraktur since it was first used for Albrecht Dürer's theoretical writings. It was designed by Johann Neudörffer the Elder (1497–1563) for the Nürnberg type cutter Hieronymus Andreä (Rösch) and cut in five sizes during the years 1522 to 1527. This page (shown in actual size) was taken from "Vier Bücher von menschlicher Proportion" ("Four Books on Human Proportions"), published in Nürnberg in 1528. Earliest and most beautiful Fraktur from which all later versions derive.

107. *Fraktur*. Dedication on the lower margin of Albrecht Dürer's drawing of the triumphal arch in honor of Emperor Maximilian I. 1518. Hand lettered (not by Dürer but probably by Johann Neudörffer, the Elder and cut in wood by Hieronymus Andreä). Somewhat reduced. Actual width of longest line: approximately 11 inches.

108. *Teuerdank-Fraktur*. Dedication to Kaiser Maximilian from "Teuerdank." Full size. Augsburg, Hans Schönsperger, 1517. The type was designed by Vinzenz Rockner, calligrapher of the Emperor (Alphabet on page 109).

109. Alphabets of the *"Gebetbuch-Type"* (prayer book) of 1514 (page 104), and the *"Teuerdank-Type"* of 1517 (page 108), both slightly reduced.

110 to 113. *Three pages from Johann Neudörffer the Elder's* manuscript "Eine gute ordnung und kurtze unterricht" ("A good primer and brief instruction"), Nürnberg 1538, and (on page 113) a "Banndtschriftlein" (a "little calligraphic ribbon") by an unknown Nürnberg calligrapher. Nürnberg, Stadtbibliothek. From "Johann Newdorffer Schreib- und Rechenmeister zu Nürnberg" (text by Gerhard Mammel, 1958), an out-of-print book which appeared in a small edition. (Reproduced with the kind permission of Mr. Rudolf Ottmann, Director of the Trade School for Graphic Arts at the Vocational School of the City of Nürnberg).

114–115. Woodcuts from the copy book of Wolffgang Fugger, "Ein nutzlich und wolgegrundt Formular Mancherley schöner schriefften...," Nürnberg, 1553. Shown here: Rotunda. Actual size.

116 and 117. *Initials and large Fraktur* from Leonhart Fuchs' "Kreüterbuch" ("Book of Herbs"), printed by Michael Isingrin, Basel, 1543. Original size.

118. *Canzley* or *Batarde* type. Page from Donatus Giano's "Respublica Venetum." Neuburg, Hans Kilian, 1557. Actual size. The headlines contain several beautiful Fraktur letters. The text is a Canzley, which was seldom used and did not become popular.

119. *Civilité*. Upper portion of a page from a "Biblia polyglotta". Antwerp, Christoph Plantin, 1596–1573. Type, actual size. The text is an especially well-designed and very well set Civilité.

120. So-called *"Manuscript Gothic,"* Copied from a 15th century French letter which first appeared in type in the "Livres d'heures" of the early French printers. The English type founder, Caslon, re-cut them in the 18th century. It is known in England and America under the names of "Old Black," "Ancient Black" and

"Black Letter." The plate here shows the re-cut by the Bauer type foundry in Frankfurt am Main. True numerals are missing; one should use those of the Caslon roman script (page 144).

121. *Schwabacher.* Belongs to the Gothic letters and descends from the late Gothic business script. Known since about 1480. The size shown on this plate is the largest of the old type size. Larger sizes are found today, but these are always new cuts. If a larger size was needed in former days, a Textur was used. To differentiate it from the "Common" or "Modern" Schwabacher – which is not an improvement – the true Schwabacher is usually called "Old Schwabacher." The "Old Schwabacher" is produced by the D. Stempel AG, Type Foundry, Frankfurt am Main.

122. *Luther Fraktur.* The Fraktur, script of the German Renaissance, was used throughout the Baroque and Rococo period without any changes. This particular cut – from the famed type foundry Egenolff-Luther of Frankfurt – is the noblest of all Fraktur letters now in existence. The plate shows the beautiful type size which was first seen in an Augsburg type specimen. Today the letter now belongs to the D. Stempel AG. Type Foundry, Frankfurt.

123. *A Roman Capital alphabet* by Giambattista Palatino. Mid-16th century. From the Ms. 5280 (G.B. Palatino, "Gran volume") of the Kunstbibliothek, Berlin-Dahlem, Arnim-Allee 23a. Reproduced with permission of Stanley Morison, Esq. from "The Monotype Recorder," April–May, 1931. Almost actual size.

124. *Centaur* by Bruce Rogers (1929) ("Monotype" 252). The famous U.S. book designer designed this beautiful roman as a careful but not pedantic adaptation of Nicolas Jenson's roman of 1470 (page 76). It is one of today's most valuable letters. The Latin verse is from Leonhard Wagner's copy book "Proba Centum scripturarum" (1517–1519), in the collection of the Bischöfliche Ordinariats-Bibliothek in Augsburg.

125. *Bembo-Roman* ("Monotype" 270). Based on the Venetian roman of Nicolas Jenson, the earliest and finest of the oldstyle roman. This specimen uses the text of Cardinal Pietro Bembo's *De Aetna,* published in 1495 in Venice by the printing and publishing house of Aldus Manutius. The script was commissioned by Manutius and cut by Francesco da Bologna: it is also called Griffo. Garamond used the script as a model for his own roman. The Bembo's capital letters are shorter than the ascenders of the lower case letters b, d, h, k, l. The slanted starting strokes are reminiscent of the oldstyle roman. The upper arm of K is slightly curved. The R has an extended end stroke. The right vertical strokes of h, n, m, incline inwards at the bottom. The Monotype Corporation Limited, London.

126. Large *Roman* from the printing shop of Jean De Tournes. The lines were taken from different titles produced by this famous printer in 1551, 1554 and 1557. Actual size. These majestic forms are the most beautiful of their kind. We do not know who cut them. They

do not seem to be by Garamond but possibly by Guillaume Le Bé I.

127. From a page of proofs in the Museum Plantin-Moretus, Antwerp. "Lettres de deux points de Petit Canon by Guillaume II Le Bé." Slightly reduced. Reproduced from J. Veyrin-Forrer et A. Jammes: "Les premiers caractères de l'Imprimerie Royale." Caractère, Noël, 1957.

128 and 129. *Garamond Roman* and *Italic.* This letter has been cut from mats which used to be credited to the "father of type founders," Claude Garamond (1480 – 1561), and are found in the collection of the Imprimerie Nationale in Paris. We now know that they are not by Garamond, but instead by the Swiss type founder and printer Jean Jannon (1580–1658). His letter, dating back to 1621, is today the most widely used representative of the oldstyle roman. Characteristic are the ascenders of letters i, m, n and r and the high cross bar of e. These are beautiful italic swash letters and ligatures. Fonderies Deberny & Peignot, Paris.

130 and 131. *Roman* by *Giovanni Francesco Gresci.* From his book "Il perfetto Scrittore," Rome, 1570. The originals are white letters on black, but the same size as those shown. The outline forms missing in the original were added by the author. A very beautiful roman face of great distinction, of a kind different from Garamond and Janson. Walter Tiemann's "Orpheus" is modeled on this.

132–135. Four pages from the writing book "Les oeuvres" by *Lucas Materot,* Avignon, 1608. The originals are copper engravings. Actual size. Materot is one of the most significant French calligraphers: all of his pages distinguish themselves by a great perfection of form and great elegance of the layout. Each of his letters is a work of art. Materot is the unsurpassed Mozart of calligraphy.

136 and 137. *Financière* (French round script). Two pages from the writing book "Les Escritures financière, et Italiene-Bastarde" by Louis Barbedor, Paris, 1646. The originals are copper etchings. Before reduction the actual height of page 136 was approximately 8 inches; and of page 137, 10½ inches. Barbedor, as important as Materot, is the master of the spirited flourish which he commands better than anyone else. The author has issued a complete facsimile edition of Barbedor's book, published by Holbein, Basel.

138 and 139. *Frieze inscription* from the façade of the Old City Hall in Leipzig, the first German city hall in the Renaissance style, designed in 1556 by Hieronymus Lotter. The inscription was originally painted. It was restored in 1672 and replaced by copper letters of the same design in 1906–09. Photo: Museum für die Geschichte der Stadt Leipzig.

140 and 141. *Janson Roman and Italic.* The Dutch version of oldstyle, which is erroneously attributed to the type cutter and type caster Anton Janson (1620–1687) of Wanden in Friesland, who, before 1669, acquired the type foundry Johann Erich Hahn in Leipzig. The typeface was actually cut in Holland about 1684 by the

Hungarian Niklaus Kis (Kis Miklòs, 1650–1702) (see Harry Carter and George Buday in "Linotype Matrix" No. 18). Even today Janson Roman and Italic have lost none of their crisp beauty and they are more valuable than ever. D. Stempel AG, type Foundry, Frankfurt am Main.

142. *Union Pearl.* This is the oldest English type of which matrices are still in existence as well as the first English ornamental script. About 1690 it belonged to the type foundry of James and Thomas Grover of London, established around 1674. Only this type size exists today. Since 1905 the plates have been owned by Stephenson, Blake & Co. of Sheffield, and for the past few years, this delightful script has been cast again. (See "The Fleuron," vol. VI, (1928) p. 110.)

143. *Numerals* from the writing book "Natural Writing" by George Shelley, London, 1709. Approximately actual size. Original is a copper engraving.

144–147. *Caslon Roman* and *Italic.* Latest historic example of the oldstyle roman. Rather conspicuous, large capitals, distinct descenders. The horizontal stroke of e is high, the a has a very large drop. The compressed, handsome italic has a number of ornamental variations.

In the Anglo-Saxon countries, Caslon has survived changing tastes and is as much appreciated today as in its youth. The original was cut by William Caslon (1692–1766) in the years between 1716 and 1728. In his cuts Caslon referred to Dutch letters. He succeeded in supplanting these on the English market with his own. These four pages show the re-cut of the Haas'sche Schriftgießerei, Münchenstein.

148 and 149. *Letra Redonda* (Spanish round script), from the book "Arte nueva de escribir" by Juan Claudio Aznar de Polanco, Madrid, 1719. Copper etching, here slightly reduced. It should certainly not be copied. But a true master could develop a modern alphabet from the letters n, o, p, l, e, i with a watchful eye to the various shapes and forms. Though most of the capitals are for us hardly legible, lower case letters have a distinct beauty.

150 and 151. *Roman and Italic by Johan Michael Schmidt.* Owned by the Bundesdruckerei (federal printing office), Berlin SW 68, Oranienstraße 91. The type cutter Johan Michael Schmidt (actually Smit), a Dutchman, was called to Berlin in 1729 by Frederic II to launch a royal type foundry. He died in 1750, probably at the age of 70. The typeface is called Dutch Medieval Roman and Italic. Its probable history: Purchased by J. L. Zingk or his heirs, thence to the Deckerschen Geheimen Oberhofbuchdruckerei (the Decker secret court printing office). This was merged in 1879 with the Royal Prussian State Printing Office, founded in 1851, which later became the Reich Printing Office, and is now the Federal Printing Office. The Schmidt typeface, still hardly known, is one of the most precious German type relics. Nine sizes were cut by Schmidt; the two largest sizes, (36 and 40 point) have the same name but were undoubtedly cut later, probably around 1813.

152 through 155. *Spanish Italic* from the book "Arte nueva de escribir..." by D. Francisco Xavier Palomares de Santiago, Madrid, 1776. Copper etching. Actual size. Very fluid broad pen script, easy to learn, and if one avoids the club-shaped thickening at the upper tip, of b d, h, l and writes the forms as in the alphabet on page 154, they would appear quite modern even today.

156. *Capitalis ombrées* by Jacques Francois Rosart (1714–1777) and *Schreibschrift* (Enschedé Nr. 90) by Joan Michael Fleischmann (1701–1768). From a book of 1766. According to Ch. Enschedé, "Fonderies de Caractères...," Haarlem, 1908. Actual size.

157. *Doubles Capitalis romaines de fantaisie* (Nr. 818), *Doubles Capitales italiques de fantaisie* (Nr. 119), *Doubles Capitales ecrites ombrées* (Nr. 820), and *Doubles Capitales romaines de fantaisie* (Nr. 821), all by Jacques Francois Rosart (1714–1777). Actual size. According to Ch. Enschedé, "Fonderies de Caractères...," Haarlem, 1908.

158. *Ornamental capitals* by Pierre Simon Fournier (1712 to 1768), Paris, Around 1735. Very slightly reduced. Louis XIV commissioned Jean Jannon (1621) to design new script types to be cut for the royal printshop. They replaced those used before – credited to Garamond, but actually scripts of Jean Jannon (1621). As a consequence of this, the other printers too demanded new scripts; Pierre Simon Fournier filled these wishes with his new roman, his italic and various ornamental scripts. Stylistically they indicate the transition from the oldstyle roman to the modern roman. The capitals, with their straight vertical and horizontal lines point the way to modern roman faces such as Walbaum.

159. *Ornamental letters* by Pierre Simon Fournier (see page 158) as used in 1788. From the collection of the author. Actual size. Fournier's ornamental scripts and decorative figures have lost none of their attractiveness.

160 and 161. So-called *Baskerville Old Face* of the type foundry Stephenson Blake & Co. of Sheffield. The script is probably not immediately linked to Baskerville (see notes on pages 162 and 163), but it is very much influenced by it. It is one of the most beautiful types of which the mats still exist, it has an incomparably different spirit than the "streamlined" re-cuts of today's Baskerville. Even keeping the general restraint of the whole in mind, the smallest curves remain extremely expressive. According to Berthold Wolpe ("Signature" No. 18), the punches were cut and shown in samples in 1776 by Isaac Moore, who came from Birmingham to Bristol.

162 and 163. *Baskerville Roman* and *Italic.* The roman and italic of the English calligrapher and printer John Baskerville (1706–1775) rest on the forms which his contemporary masters in England had given both these scripts. For some time calligraphy had developed greater differences between the thick and thin strokes than was previously practiced. Baskerville followed this new trend. In every way, his letters form the transition to the classical or modern roman, which Bodoni (see

page 172 to 175), Didot (176 and 177) and Walbaum (180 and 181) perfected at the turn of the 18th century. The stress in the curves of Baskerville's b, c, e and p is no longer as slanted as in the Garamond roman, and the upper serifs of b, d, k, l and of i, j, m, n are less slanted. The loop of g is open at left. The tail of Q in the form of a scythe. The base of E is very broad, the curve of J is flattened. The italic shows calligraphic forms of the letters J, K, N, Q, T, Y, Z, w, y, z. The beginning stroke of the italic p is lengthened. This is the new cut of the Monotype Corporation Limited of London from Baskerville types of 1760, published in 1924.

164 and 165. *Bell Roman* and *Italic* (Monotype 341). This elegant letter was cut by Richard Austin between 1787 and 1789 in London, following instructions by the enterprising publisher John Bell (1754–1831). It is of "modern" design, but its value lies in the fact that it kept the curved serifs of oldstyle, while Didot, Bodoni and Walbaum dismissed the small inner curves and made their serifs flat. This is the last roman of the transition style with particularly attractive italics. It has gentle, yet fully curved serifs. The lower arm of K is in the form of the R tail. The vertical stroke of p goes above the upper base line. The insides of O and o are still completely round, the stress is vertical, yet still gradual. Cross-bar of e is in the middle. The Monotype Corporation, Limited, London.

166. *Fry's Ornamental Number Two*. Before 1808. A delightful capital letter which first appeared in Stower's "Printer's Grammar" of 1808. The matrices are in the possession of the Stephenson, Blake & Co., Sheffield. This foundry casts not only this particular size, but also larger ones which have been cut recently.

167. *Old Face Open*. Of the same style, and probably by the same hand as the "Baskerville Old Face" as shown on pages 160 and 161. That would date it around 1760. It is the most refined letter of its kind. Owned by the Stephenson, Blake & Co. Type Foundry, Sheffield.

168 and 169. *Bulmer Roman and Bulmer Italic*, named after the English printer William Bulmer (1757–1830) who had this typeface cut for him by William Martin of Birmingham. American Type Founders Co. Inc., Elizabeth, New Jersey. Unfortunately this typeface apparently is unavailable in Europe. This is the largest size.

170. *Groote Canon Duyts* (Dutch Textur) Cut in 1748, this is one of the masterworks of the type founder Joan Michael Fleischmann (1701–1768) – born in Wöhrd near Nürnberg – who spent the better part of his life in the service of the type foundry of Izaak and Joh. Enschedé in Haarlem. This is an extremely attractive late Textur style unjustly forgotten. The letter does not contain an &. A fairly suitable & for it can be found in the Bell Italic (165).

171. *Didot Roman* of the D. Stempel AG., Type Foundry, Frankfurt am Main. Though probably not by Didot, this is an attractive form probably dating around 1810. It is related to Walbaum, a German modification of the Didot type. See also Notes to pages 176 and 177.

172. Dedication page printed by *Bodoni* in 1816. Greatly reduced. The original is about 14 inches high. Giambattista Bodoni (1740–1813), called the "king of the book printers," sought for distinct contrasts between thick and thin lines in his type. He thickened some and made others thinner than had been done before. He thus developed (around 1790) the elegant and somewhat cold modern, whose very thin serifs clearly show the influence of the lettering used by copper engravers at the time. The copper engravers had developed a "simplified" letterform to avoid turning the plate as frequently as had been necessary to engrave the serifs of oldstyle. Bodoni's new type drove out oldstyle as well as transitional styles and dominated printing until about 1850.

173. The re-cut of the *Bauer* Type Foundry of the letters in the "Manuale Tipografico" by G. B. Bodonis (1818). It is the best and most faithful interpretation of Bodoni available.

174 and 175. *Bodoni Roman* and *Italic* by the Haas'sche Type Foundry in Münchenstein. A widely used and useful interpretation, but not a faithful copy of the true Bodoni cuts (page 172). It has fine horizontal serifs and strong basic strokes. All stress in the roman – even in the curves – is precisely vertical. In the italic, too, all reminders of calligraphy have been completely eradicated. The letters *k* and *y* are exceptionally graceful.

176 and 177. *Roman* by *Firmin Didot*. The noble forms were cut around 1800 by Firmin Didot, a member of the famed French family of publishers and printers (1764–1836). They are the embodiment of Classicism and French lettering art and as beautiful today as in their time. Fonderies Deberny & Peignot, 18 rue Ferrus, Paris.

178. *Unger Fraktur*. With this late Rococo Fraktur, the Berlin book printer and type founder Johann Friedrich Unger (1735–1804) tried to achieve the elegance and clarity of roman in a Fraktur. He leaned heavily on copper-engraved Fraktur letters which had similar aims. Unger, however, got even further away from the original quill form than the engravers did. Developed in 1793, Unger's letters were not much appreciated during his lifetime, but have been widely used as book type since their rediscovery around 1910. Type Foundry D. Stempel, AG., Frankfurt am Main.

179. *Walbaum Fraktur*. This letter was cut in Weimar between the years 1803 and 1828 by J. G. Justus Erich Walbaum (1768–1839). It is to be regarded as the best late form of historic Fraktur. The difference between light and heavy strokes is emphasized. Compared to the later Fraktur of the 19th century, this portly Fraktur of the German Biedermeier period distinguishes itself by liveliness and formal opulence. H. Berthold AG., Type Foundry, Berlin.

180 and 181. *Walbaum Roman* and *Italic*. J.G. Justus Erich Walbaum (1768–1839) created with this letter the most beautiful German version of modern. In 1798 he established his own type foundry in Goslar, but in 1803 he moved to Weimar to enlarge his workshop

italic have been preserved and they are the property of H. Berthold, AG. Type Foundry in Berlin, SW 61, which donated these two pages. The serifs are thin, the basic strokes are heavy. There is a short, horizontal line between the arms of K; a flat valley of the U; only slightly rounded D curve; b, p and q have no serifs at the base. Strongly curved g loops.

182 and 183. *Gras Vibert Romain. Gras Vibert Italique.* Around 1820. Pierre Didot the Elder, opened his own Type Foundry in 1809. Following exact instructions given to him by Pierre Didot, the type founder Vibert cut news types. Among these are the Gras Vibert Romain and the Gras Vibert Italique, two complementary, almost bold, typefaces of remarkable beauty. They are owned and cast by the Deberny & Peignot, Type Foundry, Paris.

184. *Sans Serifs Shaded.* Available in 36, 30 and 14 points from Stephenson, Blake & Co., Sheffield. One of the prettiest sans serifs of the second quarter of the 19th century.

185. *Two Old Business Cards,* of the mid-19th century. Black stone gravure on white glossy cardboard. Actual size. From the author's collection. They are examples of ornamental lettering used at a time when it was considered unimaginative to start a new line with a letter style used above.

186. *Thorne Shaded.* A beautiful, shaded, outline roman by Robert Thorne of London, of same style as the bold italics on page 187. Cut around 1810. Stephenson, Blake & Co., Sheffield.

187. *Thorowgood Italic.* Bold italic of great elegance, with several decorative variations, probably cut by Robert Thorne of London whose type foundry was taken over by William Thorowgood in 1820. Stephenson, Blake & Co., Sheffield.

188. *Initiales normandes larges.* An extremely colorful, elegant French display type of the early 19th century. Fonderies Deberny & Peignot, Paris.

189. *Initiales ombrées* (1828) Classic form of a slim, bold roman. Cut around 1828. From Gille's type fonts, now with Fonderies Deberny & Peignot, Paris.

190. *Letters ombrées ornées.* Beautiful, richly ornamented letters in the Empire fashion, from the fonts of the Parisian type founder J. Gillé, presumably cut around 1810. Today the mats belong to the type foundry Deberny & Peignot, Paris. Only this (60 point) size exists.

191. *Romantiques.* Ornamental letters from the French Romantic period. The two alphabets on this page were created only 20 years after the ones on page 190. They are equally rich but decorated with entirely different design. Their effect is more bizarre. The upper alphabet, in particular, with its daring combination of two utterly different halves, is entirely romantic in spirit. Though the lower, smaller alphabet contains similarly varied form elements, the letters appear far more homogeneous than those of the upper, larger alphabet. Under the generic term *Romantiques* the Fonderie Typographique Française (Paris XV) puts out these and other letters of similar character.

192. *Bold Condensed Roman.* This typeface, called "Liliom," cut in the 19th century, is a product of the Fonderie Typographique Française, Paris XV.

193. *Egyptiennes grasses.* A good, old form of the bold Egyptian. The f and j should not be bent inwards, but should receive curves similar to those in 6. Fonderie Typographique Française, Paris XV.

194. *Bold Condensed Sans Serif.* The sans serif is a late development of modern which omits the important serifs. All strokes are optically of uniform thickness. It has existed since around 1832. Due to its tight structuring, the condensed sans serif has an almost Gothic character. Since all curves, particularly circles, are turned into long and narrow rectangles, legibility gives way to decorative appearance. The beautiful version shown here, "Antiques serrées grasses" is that of Fonderie Typographique Française, Paris XV.

195. *Ultra Bold Modern.* Also known under the name of "Normande," the Ultra Bold roman is a late development of modern, in which the basic strokes are exaggerated. Developed in the first third of the 19th century, it has great ornamental value at the expense of legibility. Fonderie Typographique Française, Paris.

196. *English Ornamental Letters* of the early 19th century. Slightly reduced.

197. *Playbill.* A 19th century "Italienne," a subspecies of Egyptian, characterized by exaggerated horizontal and weak vertical strokes. Though not exactly distinguished for legibility, this letter, like everything unusual, is very conspicuous. Should be used only for special display lines. Stephenson, Blake & Co., Sheffield.

198. *Consort Light* by the Stephenson, Blake & Co., type foundry, Sheffield. Original name: Extended Clarendon No. 2, by the defunct Type Foundry Thorowgood & Besley. Ca. 1845.

199. *Clarendon.* Clarendon is an Egyptian in which the square serifs are rounded off on the inside and which shows marked differentiation between thick and thin strokes. The fully developed "Clarendon" dates from the year 1843. The first form of this type, called "Ionic" – quite similar to the Clarendon by the Haas Type Foundry depicted here – was cast by Henry Caslon, Type Foundry, London.

200. *Anglaise (Taille-douce).* The English script, or Anglaise, derives from the English business script of the 18th century, which attained world dominance due to England's maritime position. In the beginning it was written with almost pointed quill pens; later completely pointed steel pens were used. It is difficult to draw, but it can be most charming, if well executed. It should be used only in small quantities and is unsuitable for shop and house signs. Shown here is the "Taille-douce" of the Fonderies Deberny & Peignot, 18 rue Ferrus, Paris.

201. *Ecriture italienne* from the "Traité Complet" by J. Midolle, St. Gallen, ca. 1840.

202. *French Sans Serif.* One of the common sans serifs of the 19th century, this type has numerous names, "Gothic," for one. It has a pleasant weight, good forms

and good letterspacing. Haas Type Foundry, München-stein, Germany.

203. *Extended Sans Serif*. An important display type of the late 19th century, which would require very little improvement to give it a modern look. Haas Type Foundry, Münchenstein, Germany.

204 and 205. *Gill Sans Serif*. The first sizes of Eric Gill's sans serif, the most beautiful version of all contemporary sans serifs, was put on the market in 1928. It is the only sans serif which goes back to the basic forms of oldstyle. It therefore has little in common with the sans serifs that appeared in the beginning of the 19th century, at first in England, whose forms were strongly influenced by the already degenerated late forms of modern. The lower case letters, such as a, b, e, g, r, s, t as well as the slim capital letters B, E, F, and S of the Gill remind us of the forms and proportions of oldstyle. Page 204 depicts the Gill Sans Medium. On page 205 is Gill Titling. The Monotype Corporation Limited, London.

206 and 207. *Perpetua Roman* and *Perpetua Italic* ("Monotype" 239). Master of lettering, sculptor and woodcutter, Eric Gill (1882–1940) was at one time a collaborator of Edward Johnston. He based much of this letter on stone inscriptions which he had developed in the first years of this century after much careful study of ancient letters. The endings of the E, F and T arms are almost vertical. Curved upward strokes in *B, D, P* and *R*. The curve of r ends in a short upswing. The Italic g is in the style of the Cancellaresca. The final serifs of p and q extend only at the right. The Monotype Corporation Limited, London.

208 and 209. *Weiss Roman* and *Italic*. One of the most valuable contemporary expressions of oldstyle with forceful, individualistic and spirited form. M and N are pointed at the top. The upper half of S looks larger than the lower half. The horizontal bar of e is high, d and u have an ending like a. The basic strokes of the roman are stronger at the top than at the bottom. The

beautiful italic is based on Cancellaresca. Weiss Roman was designed by Emil Rudolf Weiss (1875–1942). Bauer Type Foundry, Frankfurt am Main.

210. *Weiss-Initials, Light* by E.R. Weiss. Variations in the style of the "built-up" initials of the Middle Ages. Compare page 61. Bauer Type Foundry, Frankfurt am Main.

211. *Weiss Initials Series II* by E.R. Weiss. These capitals have a somewhat Gothic character.

212. *Graphik*. by F.H. Ernst Schneidler, Stuttgart, Bauer Type Foundry, Frankfurt am Main.

213. *Graphique* by Hermann Eidenbenz. A shaded, condensed sans serif in 19th century style (see page 194). It should only be employed for a few lines and in small quantities and must be generously spaced. Haas Type Foundry, Münchenstein.

214 and 215. *Optima*, designed by Hermann Zapf. D. Stempel AG, Type Foundry, Frankfurt am Main.

216 and 217. *Univers* designed by Adrien Frutiger. Deberny Peignot, Paris.

218 and 219. *Minerva Roman and Minerva Italic*, designed by Reynolds Stone. Linotype and Machinery Limited, London.

220. *Written Roman* based on the Humanist Antiqua, by Jan Tschichold.

221. Guide for a *contemporary handwriting* by *Alfred Fairbank*. Actual size reproductions of two plates from "The Dryad Writing Cards." (The Dryad Press, St. Nicholas Street, Leicester, England, 1946). The first edition was published prior to 1932 under the title "The Barking Writing Cards."

222. *Columna Initials* by Max Caflisch. Bauer Type Foundry, Frankfurt am Main.

223. *Romulus Initials*. The capitals of the beautiful "Romulus" by Jan van Krimpen, Haarlem. Enschedé en Zonen, Type Foundry, Haarlem.

224. *Romanée Romain & Open Initials* by Jan van Krimpen. Enschedé en Zonen, Type Foundry, Haarlem.

INDEX